Daniel Jean-Louis has a vision for the future of Haiti. With environment, and economic sustainability at the heart of this vision, he gives an optimistic account from a well-researched perspective. This book is a must-read for anyone interested in Haiti and the wider Caribbean.

—**James Ellsmoor**, *Forbes* contributor

Daniel Jean-Louis is a global thinker with heart for Haiti and all the other struggling countries around the world. His thoughtful analysis, sustainable solutions, and well-research OBED action plan will, no doubt, become a template for economic growth for years to come. *From Trade to Self-Sustainability* will encourage and direct all who want to see lasting economic reform.

—**Maarten Boute**, CEO of Digicel

From Trade to Self-Sustainability is a must-read for everyone working to improve social justice in Haiti--or anywhere else in the world. The analysis and insights are as powerful as they are unique.

—**Devin Thorpe**, *Forbes* contributor

Based on extensive research of real-world data and examples, Dr. Jean-Louis' opportunity-based economic development (OBED) approach explains how a developing country can reach its maximum potential economic growth. All who are interested in the economic health and growth of their nation will benefit tremendously from reading this book. I commend Dr. Jean-Louis' contributions to his country—Haiti—and to the field of economic development and growth.

—**Andrew Light**, Professor of Business, Liberty University

Haiti, the former *Pearl of the Caribbean*, represents an encyclopedia of "what is not working." Even after 200 years of independence, Haiti still cannot display a brochure of "what is working" from an economic development standpoint. A paradigm shift is necessary; the stakes in remaining passive or only reactive are too high for current and future generations. Proactivity via a winning strategy is necessary at all levels. Daniel Jean-Louis is proposing a disruptive alternative strategy that has a great chance for wealth creation acceleration. This book about moving from trade to self-sustainability will help countries achieve that acceleration.

—**Lesly Jules**, HOPE Haiti, Country Director

As a scholar, Dr. Daniel Jean-Louis' concepts are quantitatively and qualitatively tested and proven and should become mandatory reading in our universities. He is the epitome of a true leader.

—**Dr. Lawrence Arnold** (Major, USMC retired)

FROM TRADE TO SELF-SUSTAINABILITY

Creating Wealth to End Poverty:
OBED Principles at Work

DANIEL JEAN-LOUIS

IN COLLABORATION WITH
ANN BYLE
AND
JAN TIMOTHY SMITH

ACKNOWLEDGEMENT

I have had tremendous support and help in writing this book. It took over 2 years to do the research and one full year to do the writing and editing to the point you see now. My collaborators Ann Byle and Jan Timothy Smith have been invaluable. Very few people are as talented as they are and work as hard as they do. They have been patient, kind, and productive to get this book where it is today. They have put out their best work so this book can have the impact it needs to have in the developing world. I am very thankful for their collaboration.

I owe a great debt of gratitude to Jack and Carol Van Der Ploeg, Fred Eppright, Reagan, Stricklin, Dave Genzink, Jay Hogfelt, Bill Boesterd, Ted Boers, and Jackie Klamer. They have greatly contributed in advice, coaching, and financial support for this project to come to life.

I want to also recognize the collaboration of Lori Vandenbosch for her extraordinary service and for being so generous with her time and talent. William Overbeeke and Peter Ho have been very professional in getting the work done in very little time. I was in awe with this level of professionalism.

My gratitude also goes to Maarten Boute, Lesly Jules, Arnold Lawrence, Andrew Light, James Ellsmoor, and Devin Thorpe for their precious feedback and endorsements of this work. Their contributions have been priceless.

Many special thanks to my wife Ketia, and my children Meyer and Brianne for their support and love throughout this process. Their support has been a key factor for this book to happen.

Thank you!

FROM TRADE TO SELF-SUSTAINABILITY:
Creating Wealth to End Poverty: OBED Principles at Work

ISBN 978-1-7333116-0-1 (paperback)

For information: www.djlhaiti.com

Cover and Interior composition: Peter Ho

Printed in the United States of America

CONTENTS

FOREWORD

It seems longer than a mere seven years ago that four Americans showed up at Trinity Lodge in Port-au-Prince, Haiti. The summer of 2012 was a turning point for all of those who were there. Myself, Fred Eppright, along with my then-fiancé and now wife, Paula, my business partner Reagan Stricklin and his wife, Jennifer, were following an inexplicable heart-felt voice from a loving God to visit Haiti. That is a long story unto itself.

After an acquaintance recommended a comfortable place to stay, these four blancos rented a car at the Port-au-Prince airport and drove to Trinity Lodge. I introduced myself to the owner, Daniel Jean-Louis. This happenstance meeting was nothing short of a miracle. Since that time, a bond of friendship has evolved well beyond my capacity to understand.

The bond that holds us together is a desire to understand what has happened, and is still happening, in Haiti. Hopefully that knowledge will help start a conversation or a path to remove the current economic cloud that hovers over the country. There is no doubt in anyone's mind that Haiti is beyond an economic catastrophe. Extreme poverty is a by-product of both a dysfunctional government and a virtual collapse of any economic engine to drive the struggling economy. The government of Haiti is an integral player in perpetuating this humanitarian crisis. Whether this is out of ignorance or deliberate design is a matter of debate.

Daniel is a unique born-and-raised Haitian. His heart for his country goes beyond passion. His desire to improve current economic conditions within Haiti is the reason he lives. Daniel understands the economic damage resulting from the good intentions of many NGOs across the world. His first book, *From Aid to Trade*, was an eye opener for so many as it described what has happened to this little island nation. Hopefully it also began a thought process for world leaders. Daniel's desire is not only to begin the reconstruction of Haiti, but also to prevent this tragedy from happening again in his homeland and in countries around the world.

Daniel, Reagan, and I started Bridge Capital to try to ignite a flame in Haiti; a flame that will allow the Haitian population, the government, and non-Haitian leaders to see a way for change. This change will not happen overnight. Instead, it will be a slow process of healing, changing mindsets, and the implementation of corrective actions.

Daniel's new book, which you hold in your hands now, is the next step in trying to further the conversation about this process. Without radical change, Haiti will continue to be an open wound for the whole world to see. At some point, Haitians and non-Haitians alike will have to act. We as a global society must take responsibility and make the necessary corrective decisions and implement resulting actions. It is simply the right thing to do.

To Daniel, I want to thank you for your insight and passion to right a terrible wrong. May we all have your kind of passion within us to make this world a better place.

—**Fred Eppright**
Cofounder, Bridge Capital

INTRODUCTION

I came home to Haiti in 2006 after studying and working in the United States for some years. I left a young man unsure of my purpose and plan for my life. I came home an adult with clear eyes and clear understanding of what was happening in my homeland.

I saw an economic situation rife with unemployment and corruption, inflation, huge trade and budget deficits, and untapped resources both natural and human. The country foundered and I dreamed of doing something to help.

The business development world was the first step. I worked for Partners Worldwide, which creates partnerships and relationships among businesses to help build vital economic environments. I helped create the 100K Jobs in Haiti initiative to connect and encourage job creators in an effort to increase employment and wipe out poverty, and to help Haitian businesses rebuild after the 2010 earthquake. Partners Worldwide, myself included, spent thousands of hours training Haitians through the 100K Jobs in Haiti program but, to my dismay, those we trained were leaving the country. More than 70,000 went to Chili in 2017 alone; others went to Brazil, the Dominican Republic, French Guyana, the U.S. if they could, and other countries throughout the Caribbean. Why? Because they couldn't get jobs in Haiti.

Employment was one vital missing piece in the puzzle of Haiti's economic drama. Without better employment opportunities, Haiti would never achieve the stability and growth it needed to flourish and even survive.

As I and others watched aid organizations flood the country after the 2010 earthquake, we saw short-term help but long-term trouble. Aid groups provided goods Haitians needed such as food, water, and building materials, but often at the expense of Haitian businesses that could have provided such things. Some of those businesses were forced to close as they watched cheaper goods come into the country from abroad.

Despite all the aid, the Haitian people remained stuck in poverty. Free food and other goods helped for a short time, but what Haiti really needed was an economic renaissance that would allow businesses to invest and grow, employment to rise, and citizens to become employed at jobs with good wages. Haiti needed to move from aid-based living to sustainable economic growth.

The last several years have been even more devastating to Haiti. In a country where 59 percent of the population lives on less than $2.42 a day and what is called "unrelenting employment," Haitians and people of Haitian descent who have fled the country (or their parents did) looking for jobs are being forced to return. Neighboring Dominican Republic has expelled tens of thousands, and the United States is poised to return tens of thousands more with Temporary Protected Status (TPS).

As more and more Haitians return to a country without job opportunities and in economic peril, the country itself moves closer and closer to disaster. Imagine the toll it can take on those who return knowing they have virtually no chance of a decent job, much less a career. I felt this hopelessness myself as a young boy who knew that job and career were almost impossible to hope for. This helped birth my life quest: to end poverty in Haiti. Through this book I hope to offer a path away from the cliff of economic chaos. Overcoming this sense of hopelessness becomes more important every day to both my homeland and me.

My first book, *From Aid to Trade*, outlined a path to economic stability through a concept called Opportunity-Based Economic Development. The book's subtitle says it well: *How Aid Organizations, Businesses, and Governments Can Work Together: Lessons Learned from Haiti*. Opportunity-Based Economic Development, or OBED, offers a path to self-sustainability that taps into resources available in developing countries—Haiti included—to grow economies that support the population.

From Aid to Trade provides the conceptual framework for OBED. The book you hold translates that conceptual model into an economic model that could be quantitatively tested and proven. I put the OBED model to the test using studies, statistics, and interpretations of findings to reveal that OBED can and does help pull countries from poverty.

Our study, which is detailed in chapter 3, quantitatively tested the principles of Opportunity-Based Economic Development. According to OBED, economic development starts when assets and liabilities are turned into opportunities. In this book we will explore those claims more deeply, using examples good and not so good in Haiti and other countries.

While there has been investment in Haiti—Heineken is an example—and NGOs have started using local providers, more needs to be done. Opportunity-Based Economic Development is based on the bedrock principle that meaningful transactions—not just any transactions—build better countries. Most countries are transaction-based already, with the exception of North Korea and Cuba (though Cuba is moving toward more transactions). Revenue is generated by transactions; in healthy countries, more revenue is generated by meaningful transactions. My aim is to increase the number of meaningful transactions in Haiti and other developing countries so that growth can not only occur, but also be dramatically accelerated.

I dream of a Haiti that has moved from conducting mere transactions to instead transforming lives. I dream of a Haiti that leverages its many assets—sun, climate, beaches, affordable labor, historical significance, proximity to the United States—into meaningful transactions that generate revenue and jobs that lead to a decrease in poverty.

I'm excited to share how to do that in the pages to come.

1

FROM BALANCED TRANSACTIONS TO SUPERIOR TRANSACTIONS

Opportunity-Based Economic Development (OBED) is deeper and more nuanced than simply moving from an aid-based economy to a trade-based one. I outlined this logic in my first book with Jacqueline Klamer, *From Aid to Trade*, published in 2016. Truly OBED-based countries—those countries that pursue and practice local sourcing, platforms for connecting, advantageous policy change, and long-term investment—have taken a hard look at their assets and liabilities, and turned those things into trade opportunities that create meaningful transactions. OBED-based strategies are supported by sound legislative policies, law enforcement to prevent corruption, and investment in infrastructure such as telecommunications, roads, bridges, and ports. We called these things "opportunity-supporting factors" in *From Aid to Trade*.

Now let's move deeper into OBED thinking and take a closer look at balanced transactions—the basis for all business—and superior transactions, the goal of OBED. Balanced transactions are defined as transactions in which businesses (supply) make a profit and the customer (demand) is satisfied.

A customer visits the bakery and buys two loaves of bread. The bakery makes a small profit and the customer's needs are satisfied. A driver pulls into a gas station and fills his motorbike with gasoline. The station makes a profit on the gasoline, and the driver is free to drive another couple of days. You hire the neighborhood teenager to mow your lawn, paying him for his work. All these balanced transactions are normal and good and are the desired goal of OBED. However, unbalanced transactions can occur, resulting in poverty creation and asset dissolution.

From Aid to Trade introduced OBED as the "means [of] harnessing assets and capital through entrepreneurial opportunities to increase balanced transactions."[1] Individuals and businesses pursue these opportunities to turn assets and liabilities into goods and services that meet demands and make a profit. OBED promotes the use of balanced transactions as the best way to fulfill needs in the society.

OBED is specifically tailored to underdeveloped or struggling countries, like Haiti, and offers strategies that can be implemented almost immediately by businesses, individuals, governments, and NGOs, and can expand to include whole sectors of the economy. Creating balanced transactions is the means to the end goal of creating wealth through alignment of all players in the economy, from NGOs to governments, from small businesses to large ones.

In *From Aid to Trade* we offer several examples of countries that have turned assets and liabilities into marketable opportunities. Brazil has turned its vast natural resources—beaches, rainforests, agricultural land—into market growth that shot it to the top of economically sound countries around the world.[2] Russia used legislation—after the end of the USSR—to help privatize a number of sectors and restore a free-market economy.[3] India used its growing population to create opportunity for foreign investment in customer service and information technology.[4]

China at first saw its 1.3 billion people as a liability, with rural Chinese often living in poverty. Thanks to government planning, the country became a more free-market economy and encouraged foreign business to invest in industries that used the vast numbers of rural Chinese as cheap labor. We won't go into the issues surrounding China and its repressive policies, but the country did leverage what many perceived as a liability into an asset and raised many out of poverty.[5]

Post-apartheid South Africa used its environmental assets to grow its tourism industry, and natural resources to grow its mining and industry sector.[6] Each of these countries, together known as BRICS, has moved forward to create environments for balanced transactions that grew the economy and improved the financial status of many of its people.

From Aid to Trade also outlined five steps to moving successfully from an aid-based economy to a trade-based one. Haiti, which has at its core a market-based economy, has been hampered by a number of issues including corruption, political instability, and a huge number of aid organizations—NGOs, non-government organizations—that undermine the market-based system. There are up to 20,000 NGOs in Haiti alone.[7] Often these NGOs, instead of purchasing goods and services inside Haiti, import those same goods and services. Balanced transactions fly out the window as donations negate the need for trade. (Why would you start or continue a bottled-water business in Haiti when bottled water is provided for free by numerous NGOs?) In fact, dependence on aid moves countries away from their wealth-creation goals. OBED thinking, however, takes a country from dependence on aid to creating balanced transactions and thus creating wealth, the underlying theme of this book.

The key driving factor to growth and change is the availability of marketable and viable business transactions. Once that base is in place, a number of sustaining factors keep the market economy moving: rule of law, innovation, trade policies, infrastructure, professional development opportunities, education, environmental stability, and gender equality.[8]

MOVING FROM "FINE" TO "GREAT"

These factors are dissected in *From Aid to Trade*. Now, however, it's time to move beyond simply describing OBED and describing lessons learned and knowledge gained. It's time to take OBED principles and use them to study countries that practiced those principles and saw growth, and apply them to countries seeking to build strong and successful market-based economies.

I want to expand the logic of OBED. OBED is more than turning aid to trade through balanced transactions. Countries can engage in balanced transactions every day and do fine. I want countries, using OBED strategies, to move beyond simply "fine" to "great." I want developing countries to move beyond balanced transactions to superior transactions because, by doing so, countries position themselves to create wealth faster. By creating wealth faster, countries can make the leap from poverty to wealth that much quicker. Superior transactions create more wealth, faster.

A superior transaction is a balanced transaction that provides superior returns to both sides of the transaction, as well as provides taxes returned to the government, which then uses those taxes in a healthy way.

Balanced transactions occur routinely; superior transactions aren't always so routine. Every business that wants to survive strives for good customer service. Those that want to thrive strive for an added sparkle that brings customers back again and again. They strive to be superior.

WHAT "SUPERIOR" LOOKS LIKE: WHITE MOUNTAIN PUZZLES

My friend Ann, a substantial contributor in writing this book, is a puzzler and is partial to White Mountain puzzles. She can buy a White Mountain puzzle at a number of retailers in her area, which she has occasionally done. She walks in, checks out the limited selection of puzzles, and chooses one. She pays for it along with the other items in her cart, which likely includes groceries, cleaning supplies, and health/beauty items.

Ann also shops for puzzles on the White Mountain website. She can look at the list of puzzles she's already purchased, scroll through the newest puzzles, check out the sale puzzles, and take advantage of offers such as Buy 3, Get 1 Free. Once she chooses and orders, an email arrives saying her order has been received.

A second email arrives in another day or so saying her puzzles are about to ship; another email says they have shipped and when to expect them. Each email is from a named customer service representative.

Recently Ann sent a return email asking about tours of the company because she was considering a vacation in that area of the country. Within minutes an email came back from Cathy saying she's sorry they don't do tours but they do have a great gift shop. Another time Ann ordered a puzzle she already had. When she called to ask about how to return the unopened puzzle, the customer service person said, "Just keep it; gift it to someone who loves puzzles." She did and that person was thrilled. Both she and White Mountain shared their superior transaction with someone who could benefit.

One time a package of puzzles arrived with an extra in the box, one Ann hadn't ordered. She called to ask about returning the puzzle that had gotten in the box by mistake. The customer service representative assured her there was no mistake. The shipment had been delayed, so White Mountain sent that extra puzzle as a gift to say "thank you for waiting."

The first puzzle purchase at the retail store was a balanced transaction. The second puzzle purchase was a superior transaction because Ann was more than satisfied and will be back to order via the website (and probably visit the puzzle store on vacation), and is willing to pay shipping costs because of the superior benefits of buying directly from the company. White Mountain will get repeat business because of its superior customer service.

Now take those transactions and magnify them to the size of a country. Imagine multiple businesses willing to do what it takes to ensure that customers are highly satisfied. Some businesses can spend $100 to create a product to sell; those businesses can sell that product for $100 and break even, offering only mediocre customer service. But what if that business wants to offer great customer service in return for selling products for $120? That's a superior transaction.

VERY SATISFIED CUSTOMERS + PROFIT + TAX DOLLARS = A GROWING ECONOMY

A business can transact all day long and provide marginal value-added and adequate satisfaction. Unless a business is willing to think outside the box to maximize how it transforms its assets, as well as think about what the customer needs and desires, that business will achieve only at a marginal level. But think about the possibilities of offering superior satisfaction (demand) for a superior price (supply). (Remember that a "superior transaction" is one in which the supplier makes a good profit, the customer is very satisfied, and the government gains from tax dollars.) Superior transactions hinge on the willingness of a customer to be more satisfied and the willingness of a business to offer that satisfaction.

Multiply by billions of dollars' worth of superior transactions; the economy grows as customers grow more satisfied. A country can get by if its businesses get by at a minimum level. A country is wealthy if its businesses are wealthy. Imagine a country in which businesses—and the government itself—strive for superior transactions in every arena.

My goal with *From Trade to Self-Sustainability* is to encourage individuals, businesses, entrepreneurs, governments, and NGOs to engage in superior transactions. My goal is to help countries put OBED strategies to work for them.

THE ETHIOPIA EXAMPLE

Ethiopia, the second most populous nation in Africa, saw steady annual economic growth starting in the 2000s. It was one of the fastest-growing countries among IMF member countries.[9] While it remains one of the poorest countries,[10] it is seeing much growth in agriculture, construction, and services, with growth also in manufacturing.[11]

Ethiopia has taken one of its liabilities—trash in its capital city of Addis Ababa—and turned that liability into an asset. The garbage that filled the streets was turning Addis Ababa into a disaster of litter, smell, vermin, and disease. The East Africa country partnered with Cambridge Industries to build the Reppie Waste Facility. Now all that garbage is collected and burned, which boils water to create steam, which turns a turbine generator to create electricity. Cambridge estimates the facility will burn 80 percent of the city's trash to meet 25 percent of the city's energy needs.[12]

Ethiopia, a country once marked by famine, is now known for economic progress. A city once known for its trash is now becoming known for its business development.

This is an example of OBED thinking in action. The basic premise of OBED is that economic development should come from the available opportunities in a country. In Ethiopia, one of those opportunities is trash. While many may see trash as a liability, the value of OBED thinking is that even liabilities can become marketable opportunities and avenues for growth.

Ethiopia moved far beyond making balanced transactions with its trash. Balanced transactions would have meant simply recycling the trash, placing it in landfills, and/or creating fertilizer. These would have been the usual paths of balanced transactions. However, the country transformed a highly toxic liability (trash) into a superior transaction for a high-level consumer need (electricity). Ethiopia made the best out of a devastating situation by solving one of its most pressing needs. Examples like this one need to be multiplied over and over by struggling and developing countries.

TURNING ASSETS INTO OPPORTUNITIES

OBED means harnessing assets and capital through entrepreneurial opportunities to increase superior transactions. Countries have many assets; turning those assets into opportunities is the key to growth and wealth. The principal agents that transform assets and liabilities into economic opportunities are enterprises and entrepreneurs. OBED's ultimate goal is to foster the development of resource generators—enterprises and entrepreneurs—to spur economic growth.

According to OBED strategy, assets in themselves do not boost economic growth. Those assets need to be transformed into economic opportunity. Businesses and entrepreneurs must take those assets and turn them into viable market opportunities before the assets can create value. The move from balanced transactions to superior transactions can have a direct effect on economic growth. Yet those assets must have market capability, and a country must have the resources to transform those assets to produce competitive advantage. Once that competitive advantage is there, superior transactions result.

Two hundred years ago, countries with rich oil deposits had no way to use those assets (and didn't know they were assets). Today, oil is liquid gold. Two hundred years ago, a country's richest assets may have been agricultural land to plant crops to feed its people and sea ports to export the extra foodstuffs. Now, thanks to technology, agricultural land isn't the asset it once was. The strength of a country's assets isn't bound by time; it's bound by what consumers are willing to pay for that asset now and in the future.

When developing countries prioritize assets based on customer preference, this provides a higher competitive advantage for businesses to produce superior transactions. These superior transactions then positively impact the economy in general.

UNTAPPED ASSETS: HAITI AND CONGO

OBED principles work. Poor countries haven't transformed their assets into enough opportunities; wealthier countries have. Poor countries may have a good number of balanced transactions going on at sector and national levels, but those transactions haven't made the leap to become superior transactions that lead to increased wealth for individuals, businesses, and the country at large.

Haiti, my own country, has had trouble transforming its assets into meaningful, superior transactions. We have thousands of miles of beaches that could draw tourism dollars from abroad, but those beaches for the most part are unused while tourist dollars go to neighboring Dominican Republic. The DR has seen a 6.4 percent increase in foreign visitors as recorded in 2016, which has generated revenues estimated at $6.8 billion.[13] Haiti, on the other hand, reported a 14.5 percent drop in foreign visitors in 2016, mostly attributed to political turmoil.[14]

Our beaches are inaccessible by road, have no amenities, and are often dirty. Yet those beaches, a huge asset to Haiti, could be transformed into economic opportunity with investment in buildings, roads, and other infrastructure, as well as avenues to attract tourists. Haiti has other assets as well, including a cheap labor force and a rich history that could be turned into tourism opportunities. Yet those assets sit largely unused and untapped.

The Democratic Republic of Congo, the second poorest country in the world behind only Central African Republic,[15] (Haiti is 17th) is in an acute, chronic economic depression in light of recent drops in worldwide oil prices. Low oil prices, massive debt, and government weakness are hurting the economy.[16] One of Congo's biggest assets is its natural resources, including iron ore. Turning an asset such as iron ore into market opportunities with superior transactions could be key to improving Congo's economy. This is a prime example of the fact that the mere presence of an asset is no guarantee of economic growth and wealth creation.

Transaction-based economies are not new; countries around the world have been transacting for generations and continue to do so today. The exceptions, communist Cuba and North Korea, are slowly adjusting their economies to the free market system, and China has successfully done so despite keeping its communist political system.

My first book, *From Aid to Trade*, highlighted the need for countries to increase opportunities to transact by turning their assets and liabilities into marketable opportunities and balanced transactions. Economies grow one transaction at a time; increasing balanced transactions yields increased economic value. But there is so much more to transactions as I will explain in greater detail when I introduce our OBED research study in chapter 3. By studying the strength of their assets, countries can specialize and prioritize assets with the highest potential to generate revenue and thus maximize their opportunities.

Think about it: Why would a business make a 10 percent profit in exchange for just 5 percent customer satisfaction, when they could make 30 percent profit and have a 15 percent customer satisfaction rate? By increasing both profit and customer satisfaction, the transaction moves from a balanced transaction to a superior one. Countries can accumulate wealth exponentially and at an accelerated rate when balanced transactions move into the superior category. This is the heart of OBED.

Our research study, which looked at thirty-eight countries, proves that OBED concepts can work for all developing countries. Each of the thirty-eight countries we studied has adapted OBED principles, thus upgrading the economy and raising millions out of poverty. Sadly, many countries are stuck in their minimally beneficial market system, settling for a limited number of balanced transactions across just a few sectors. They remain burdened by poverty and unemployment because they have not maximized the return on their assets and liabilities. Their many assets remain sadly untapped.

An inspiring example of a country that has moved from balanced transactions to superior transactions in a relatively short period of time is South Korea. Let's look at it now.

SOUTH KOREA–FROM SUBJECT TO TRADE KINGDOM

South Korea has a rich history of culture and, too often, military action. Its modern history, for our purposes, begins with the country's annexation by Japan in 1910. Several independence movements took place, including the March First Movement in 1919 and another in 1931. During World War II, the Japanese used the Korean people in its war machine in a variety of unpleasant ways.

The Korean provisional government, located in China, declared war on Japan in December 1941 and organized an army in China that fought with the Allies until the Japanese surrender in 1945.

Korea was to be divided between four Allies: the U.S., England, China, and the U.S.S.R. With Russia advancing into the region, it was decided that the Korean peninsula be divided at the infamous 38th parallel, with the U.S controlling the southern portion.

It wasn't long before the Russians made a move to annex the southern part of the peninsula, causing the southern people to form an army and wage war on the north, with the help of U.S. military forces. China got involved, the U.N. got involved, casualties mounted, and rhetoric flew. Finally, in July 1953, the war ended and the peninsula was divided.[17] South Korea was devastated, its land ruined by war and its people shattered. Foreign aid poured in.

By 1960, South Korea was one of the poorest countries in the world and heavily dependent on foreign aid. In terms of disposable income, its rate was lower than Haiti, Ethiopia, Yemen, and India.[18] Its military government, however, worked hard at developing the economy, which grew an average 9 percent annually, with per capita income increasing more than a hundred times.[19] The population grew, education levels increased, infrastructure was stabilized, businesses were started, and people migrated from the rural areas to big cities for jobs. With the exception of 1980, the South Korean economy grew every year, thanks to a huge increase in the Manufacturing sector.[20]

The Asian Crisis of 1997–1998 nearly brought South Korea, Thailand, and Malaysia to their knees after years of economic growth. The crisis disclosed weaknesses—first revealed in Thailand and then its neighbors—that included slowing export growth, huge deficits, foreign borrowing in the private sector, an inflated real estate market, and an unsupervised banking sector, among others.[21]

Yet South Korea found its way out of that crisis by taking necessary steps to fix its weaknesses and grow its economy. Today's current troubles, including corruption scandals and pollution, are causes for caution, but they don't negate the economic growth that brought South Korea from a war-torn disaster to one of the top economies in the world in less than sixty years. South Korea is a prime example of OBED strategies at work.

The biggest thing South Korea did was move from balanced transactions to superior transactions in a planned and measured way. From the late 1950s to the early 1980s, percentages of several key sectors in the nation's economy switched importance. The

Agriculture, Forestry, and Mining sectors declined from 40 percent of economic activity in 1962–64 to 13.5 percent in 1982–86. Manufacturing rose from 12 percent to 30.2 percent during that time. Utilities and Construction, and Services both rose during that time as well.[22]

South Korea moved from an agricultural-based economy to a manufacturing-based economy. Within the Manufacturing sector (a sub-sector of Industry), the country moved from low-yield industries such as textile and garments to higher-yield markets such as electronics and steel.[23] This is classic OBED strategy: move from balanced transactions (garment, textiles) to superior transactions (electronics, steel). South Korea would have plodded along nicely with its textile manufacturing, but instead chose to sprint ahead by manufacturing higher-yield goods.

Another move the country made was diversifying its markets from consumer goods to capital goods (goods used to manufacture other goods, rather than being bought by end-use consumers). Iron, steel, petrochemicals, metals, and refined oil were the bases for other heavy industry such as shipbuilding, automobiles, and large construction products such as machine tools and heavy equipment.[24] The smaller industries were still present, but South Korea moved to include capital goods in its portfolio. It moved from balanced transactions into even more superior transactions.

South Korea also used its governmental power to implement policies, reforms, incentives, and strategies to build the businesses and sectors that brought the most growth and wealth to its people. This is another OBED strategy put into practice. South Korea targeted industries that would likely play a key role in growing its international markets and created incentives to foster that growth. If a sector began to falter, the government would step in to help boost that area.[25]

The government's nimble and fluid policy making led to an increase in superior transactions. The government also fostered the South Korean value of education, which allowed the country to move with ease into industries that required skilled workers,[26] yet another OBED bedrock.

There is much more to the story of South Korea's economic rise, its stumbles, and its continued success in the modern world economy. This brief picture, however, points to the success that using OBED strategies can bring.

My goal for this book, and my heart's goal for developing countries, is to help them learn the lessons of OBED and, like South Korea, begin transforming assets and liabilities into market opportunities that yield superior transactions, which leads to increased wealth at all levels. Next, let's look more closely at specific ways we can encourage economic growth: proven strategies I call "wealth accelerators."

2

WEALTH ACCELERATORS IN OPPORTUNITY-BASED ECONOMIC DEVELOPMENT (OBED)

We are now ready to move into the meat of what it means to move from balanced transactions to superior transactions, the fastest and surest way to go from trade-based economies to self-sustainability. So far we have established that to go from trade to self-sustainability, superior transactions are required to enhance existing or not-yet-existing balanced transactions.

Transaction enhancement—moving from balanced to superior transactions—can happen in a variety of ways. One way is that the transaction itself gets bigger and better; that is, instead of trading ten cords of wood to one supplier, an entrepreneur trades a hundred cords of wood to four suppliers, one of which also buys the wood chips created when trees are prepared for shipping.

Another way to enhance transactions is to use better strategies to increase transactions while keeping fixed costs or capital investments the same. A company may use advances in technology to increase factory output by double, triple, or even quadruple using the same machines and number of workers. Balanced transactions have become superior ones at that factory.

We want to address here the means by which countries and businesses can transform assets and liabilities—its balanced transactions—into superior transactions and thus increase productivity and wealth. I call this activity *wealth creation acceleration*, and the strategic means to do this activity I call "wealth accelerators."

Wealth accelerators take a country's balanced transactions and enhance them so they become superior transactions. Or it could be that an entrepreneur uses wealth accelerators to double, triple, or even quadruple the number of transactions using the same fixed costs or capital investment.

Balanced transactions, however, don't disappear. They are still there, but maturing into superior transactions via wealth acceleration tools. Think of it as adding baking powder to a recipe for yeast bread. The yeast is there to facilitate the bread rising and does its job; but the baking powder enhances the rising power of the yeast to create even bigger bread.

A factory, for example, produces 100 units of a particular product. With a wealth accelerator such as a loan or a private investment, that factory owner could purchase another machine to add another 200 units to its production numbers. Without that enhancement, the factory is still transacting. With it, the factory is producing at superior numbers. In this chapter and throughout the book, you will see numerous examples of how assets and liabilities are enhanced to yield more wealth faster.

Wealth Accelerators

Geographic location
Natural resources
Multilateral trade opportunities
Cultural history
Labor pool
Machinery and robotics
Information technology
Value chain optimization
Private equity investment
Foreign Direct Investment (FDI)
Credit system

Wealth accelerators are richly varied and cover a broad range of options, briefly explained here.

Credit system—banks extend credit to businesses large and small to allow them to expand and diversify. A company has $100,000 but needs $150,000 to expand; instead of getting that additional $50,000 from an investor who then controls a portion of the company, the company borrows against the $100,000 in equity and gets to keep control. The cost to the company is the payable interest, which can vary depending on the risk level present in a specific situation.

The ratio of a company's loan capital (debt) to the value of its common stock (equity) is called leverage; the expectation is that the profits raised using the borrowed capital will be greater than the interest paid on it. Credit can be extended through retail banking and credit unions, which also uses the company's money to create additional transactions for its own use. It's the lending principle that says a dollar is owned by one entity (you) but lent out by a second entity (the bank) to create wealth for itself.

Private equity investment—privately-owned businesses and/or individuals invest in a private business; this non-lending arrangement doesn't pay interest because the investment isn't a loan. The investor becomes part owner of the company.

Large companies can raise capital through an IPO (initial public offering), in which investors buy shares and are able to trade shares among themselves. Investors then earn dividends off the profit a company makes. Companies can offer a certain number of shares to raise a certain amount of money. In 2004, Google's IPO stock price was $85. According to Fortune, the company's stock now is worth 22 times what it cost in 2004.[27] Google used the influx of cash to expand its operations.

There are many financial instruments within the equity and debt market available for companies large and small looking for private equity investments. Among them: investment bankers, private investors, investment companies, bonds, letters of credit, cash, negotiable bills, money market accounts, securities, hedge market funds, and others.

Foreign Direct Investment (FDI)—an investment made by an individual or business based in one country into an enterprise in another country; often this involves ownership or controlling interest in that business. For example, an investor from China builds and owns a factory in the United States; or a Canadian company builds and owns a plant in Mexico. Countries, businesses, and individuals are competing for FDI, searching for foreign investors with private capital. The investor makes money, the country in which investment occurs takes in more taxes, more jobs become available, and wealth accrues.

Countries receiving the most FDI in 2017 were the United States at $311 billion and China at $144 billion. Also on the list are Hong Kong, Netherlands, Ireland, Australia, Brazil, Singapore, France, and India.[28]

Value chain optimization—process by which a company adds value to a product, including production, distribution, and customer service before and after sale. Michael Porter developed the idea of value chain in the 1985 book *Competitive Advantage*, in which he explained that a value chain "is a collection of activities that are performed by a company to create value for its customers."[29] Businesses that adapt a *Competitive Advantage* attitude, mindset, and action plan are more inclined to optimize the many ways to transform assets and liabilities into superior transactions.

Consider Netflix, once a business that mailed DVDs of movies and TV shows to its subscribers. When internet use became widespread, Netflix moved to offering an online video streaming service. Now Netflix is producing its own movies and shows, using its already-established online platform to distribute those shows. Also consider the dairy company that used to buy milk from farmers and cheese from cheese makers to sell to its customers. That dairy company adds to its value chain when it purchases its own cows and machinery, allowing it to process the milk and make its own cheese to sell to customers. Each of these businesses used its competitive advantage—distribution platforms and customer base—to create superior transactions that build wealth.

These examples of optimized value chains are instructive to developing countries; businesses can be more successful when they optimize the value chain where they have the competitive advantage. However, if a business has a competitive advantage and doesn't use it, that business loses. The business may stay at usual levels (balanced transactions), which is a loss when considering what it could be doing via value chain optimization (superior transactions). Developing countries can trade acceptably, but can't move to self-sustainability if they don't optimize value chain and increase superior transactions.

Machinery and robotics—manufacturing capability at a business or in a country using equipment already in place or readily available. Before the Industrial Revolution, people produced goods by hand and lived in a primarily agrarian society. As the population increased and strides were made in the technology of the day, more and better machinery allowed businesses (and countries) to increase output dramatically to provide for needs in the country of origin and to export.

Machinery and robotics amplify production, allowing companies to scale and reduce the cost per unit produced. The cost per unit goes down as production numbers rise. Goods can move from China to the United States, for example, at cheaper cost because of the huge number of goods produced. Machinery and robotics that reduce production times also allows countries or businesses to sell more because they produce more.

Developing countries don't have the ability to scale because they don't have the machinery, the capital to add or upgrade that machinery, or the know-how to implement changes needed to scale products. These countries are missing out on much wealth creation by not being able to turn balanced transactions into superior transactions through the wealth accelerator of machinery.

Labor pool—the supply of skilled and unskilled workers to fill positions at all levels of an enterprise. A country's labor pool, particularly in the developing world, has been an accelerator for companies specializing in light manufacturing such as textiles. Low-priced consumer goods such as T-shirts, underwear, and other clothing require higher numbers of low-cost workers and higher manufacturing needs. Bangladesh, Haiti, and Nicaragua are tapping into a plethora of low-cost workers as wealth accelerators in the textile industry to pull themselves out of poverty.

However, countries should not depend only on a low-cost labor pool as a wealth accelerator. High-skilled workers, particularly with knowledge of technology and communications, attract FDI and local investment and can draw specialized businesses to a country. A high-skill labor force allows companies to diversify into research and development as well as explore new market opportunities to service existing markets on a higher scale. A nation's GDP per capita rises because it can produce more high-end goods that make more money.

A country using its labor force in diverse ways can turn balanced transactions into superior ones. All levels of manufacturing needing workers of all skill levels lead to a highly diversified economy and more wealth creation.

Information technology—access to telecommunications networks, internet services, technical machinery, satellite technology, computers, and other forms of technology. IT allows the world to be connected and allows businesses to expose their goods and services to a worldwide audience in a short amount of time. Competitive advantages result, including the ability to bypass intermediaries and reach the consumer directly. Businesses can scale higher and better when they can introduce products directly to the buyer.

This ability to reach consumers directly has turned bookselling, the music business, and retail stores on their collective ears. Bookstores from large chains to small indies are closing as customers buy from online retailers or directly from the publisher; publishers are trying to reach more consumers directly to grab sales that have been going to online retailers such as Amazon.

Music giants Taylor Swift, Katy Perry, and Beyoncé are releasing their albums and singles directly to consumers, thereby avoiding costly intermediaries that can control pricing, content, and distribution avenues, and take a cut of the profits. Huge retail outlets such as Sears and Toys R Us have closed as customers take to the internet to shop.

IT allows businesses to build a platform—website, e-commerce outlet, payment platform—relatively cheaply and through it connect directly to the consumer. It also allows research to move at the speed of the internet, makes sharing information easier and faster, and facilitates quick fulfillment (think Amazon during holiday seasons!).

Multilateral trade opportunities—relationships with other countries with which businesses or countries trade. Countries can use multilateral trade opportunities as wealth accelerators when they enter into agreements that allow businesses to export their goods at cheaper prices to countries looking for those goods, and import goods that are made cheaper elsewhere. Having a trade agreement allows both countries to plan their trades to optimize the creation of economic value added for both. Countries typically use tariffs and quotas to control their imports and allow for local markets to meet some of those needs.

Cultural history—historic sites such as battlefields, ruins, relics, churches, shipwrecks, homes, and other important places to a country's origins and history. Digging into a country's past can unveil tremendous opportunities for tourism companies to maximize those assets into productive, meaningful, and superior transactions. Boston, Massachusetts, in the United States has literally embedded its history into the sidewalks by creating the Freedom Trail that leads visitors to sixteen historic sites around the city, including the Paul Revere House, Bunker Hill Monument, and the USS *Constitution*.

Some cities and countries have done a much better job of turning historic sites and facts into superior transactions than others. Countries such as Haiti have had their colonial churches and artifacts destroyed in riots and protests, thus diminishing opportunities for tourists. Haiti also lets its historic resources go to waste. For instance, Christopher Columbus landed for the first time in the New World at Mole St Nicholas in Haiti's northwest region. Visiting this area requires eight hours of driving on wild roads only accessible by four-wheel-drive vehicles. Upon arrival, there are only declining vestiges of the enormous ruins that show signs of obvious neglect.

Imagine if carloads and shiploads of tourists were visiting the site of Christopher Columbus's landing, creating the demand for hotels, transportation, restaurants, and souvenir shops. All these transactions could spur growth particularly at a sectoral level. On the other hand, think about Grand Canyon National Park in the American Southwest, which drew 6.25 million visitors in 2017.[30] It's easy to see the comparison and know which country is creating superior transactions based on cultural and natural history.

Natural resources—oil, ores, minerals, fossil fuels, gemstones, timber, water, sunlight, wind, fast-running rivers, sea life, wildlife. The southern African country of Botswana is rich in natural resources and has tapped into that sector to increase its wealth. Mining brings in about a third of all government revenue. Diamonds are the main commodity, though Botswana also mines nickel-copper, coal, soda ash, gold, silver, semi-precious stones, and granite.[31] Profits from mining are fed into education and other services, in part making this country one of the success stories of the developing world.

Geographic location—located on important trade routes, has large rivers, deep water ports, access to fresh water, or have land features such as mountains, plains, farmland or rain forests, etc. Like all assets, these need to be transformed through innovative leadership, wealth acceleration tools, and vision for them to yield economic benefit. Switzerland, for instance, has turned its location in the heart of the Alps into an asset by offering ski vacations at a multitude of resorts, as well as tapped other winter sports that take advantage of the mountainous location. It would be silly for Switzerland to try to sell tourists on a seaside vacation, just as it would be ridiculous for a Caribbean island with miles of beaches to sell tourists on a ski vacation. Geography, with the help of wealth accelerators, can yield superior transactions. Many developing countries do not turn geographic location into superior transactions, or many times any transactions at all.

Haiti is located just 800 miles from the southern coast of the United States, yet receives very little benefit from that nearness in the form of export opportunities or tourism dollars from U.S. visitors. Haiti has not turned the wealth accelerator of geographic location into marketable opportunity.

Countries such as Chad in Africa are landlocked, which eliminates opportunities brought about by ports. Other countries have these assets but take little advantage of them. Like all assets, geographic location needs to be developed and transformed to create wealth.

ASSET MULTIPLICATION

As we have already seen, simply possessing an asset doesn't mean growth is the result. In our research we found that successful countries have *developed* their assets and liabilities and used wealth accelerators to create a long succession of superior transactions in the most viable sectors, which in turn creates economic growth and wealth accumulation at a national level.

Another aspect of OBED that plays into a country's success is the ability to combine multiple developed assets to create more impact through superior transactions. We call it *asset multiplication*. Once a country learns how to develop, combine, and multiply assets using wealth accelerators, superior transactions result and wealth grows. Balanced transactions produce a multiplied effect; superior transactions produce an exponential effect.

Developing countries are doing a lot of balanced transactions, but those countries have not used enough wealth accelerators to turn those balanced transactions into superior ones. Come with me to look more closely at how to combine wealth accelerators.

Asset Multiplication
Combining Wealth Accelerators

COMBINING WEALTH ACCELERATORS

As a country considers its assets, liabilities, and wealth accelerators, it must look hard at how to combine those things to create even more impact. For developing countries, finding new and unique ways to create and enhance superior transactions will lead inevitably to increased wealth.

Let's look at a historical example of this idea. The H.J. Heinz Pickling Company wanted to expand is pickle business back in 1896 and looked at Holland, Michigan, as a possible site. The company needed cucumbers to turn into pickles; specifically, it needed 30,000 bushels of cucumbers, which meant roughly 300 acres each yielding 100 bushels per acre. Local farmers committed to planting 500 acres of cucumbers on land perfect for that crop.[32]

The farmers also offered $2,500 to help Heinz buy property along Lake Macatawa to build a deep-water dock to expedite shipping into Lake Michigan and, thus, huge cities such as nearby Chicago.[33] Heinz bought produce from local farmers, who had invested money and land to create an excellent climate for Heinz. The company also employed many workers from its beginnings to the present, including up to a thousand during the Depression, German prisoners-of-war due to local labor shortages, and people of Hispanic descent who had only been allowed to work in the fields.[34]

Farmers leveraged their land, agricultural expertise, and money to help bring a profitable business to their area. The city of Holland provided laws and infrastructure to benefit the business. Heinz in turn bought cucumbers from local farmers and turned them into pickles, hired local workers, and brought taxes into the local government that helped provide schools, roads, harbors, electricity, and other infrastructure needs.

Each player in this scenario used an asset or assets to create superior transactions that benefited all, and continues to do so today at the plant in Holland. Instead of farmers being content with only farm-to-table transactions, which they continued to do, they were able to increase their impact by adding manufacturing, transportation, distribution, and retail to the value chain. Superior transactions occurred in each of these areas, bringing wealth to many businesses and individuals. The effect on the community and Heinz was superior.

There are many combinations of wealth acceleration tools countries can use. A country rich in wildlife could entice foreign investment to help build lodges and purchase vehicles to create a safari tourism business, which could advertise using social media platforms and be paid for through banking institutions. Each step in this process can yield superior transactions.

Cheap labor may be plentiful, as is farmland and deep-water ports. Agribusiness concerns may use that cheap labor to prepare crops such as corn, coffee, or soybeans for shipping to neighboring countries; it may also use that cheap labor to create and package goods for shipping abroad using machinery available in port cities. Farming, manufacturing, transportation, and natural resources are all tapped for superior transactions.

A country rich in skilled labor and a technology infrastructure may lure foreign investment in customer service centers that field calls from all over the world, or that supply technology support for neighboring countries. Assets are used to create superior transactions.

The key is getting the most out of a country's assets and liabilities using wealth acceleration tools to their highest capacities to create superior transactions. This is the foundational truth of Opportunity-Based Economic Development.

Accelerators in the financial arena include private capital investment, FDI, credit via the banking system, and leverage. A country can use a combination of these tools to create superior transactions.

Costa Rica has long been attracting Foreign Direct Investment (FDI), particularly in the early years of the new millennia. Costa Rica has made a concerted effort to court FDI, including from China, India, the United States, and other countries.[35] This yielded agreements with the U.S., membership in the Central American Free Trade Agreement, and an agreement with the European Union.[36]

Costa Rica's president actively sought FDI from China, with China's FDI now exceeding $500 million.[37] Costa Rica also began simplifying its regulatory structure and requirements, and began offering up its highly educated workforce as an incentive.

"Costa Rica also offers several advantages not found in some other frontier markets, such as a stable political environment, democratic institutions, unfettered repatriation of profits, and policy predictability—meaning freedom from sudden changes," according to author Al Emid.[38]

This Central American country used FDI as a wealth accelerator to draw additional business to the country, including Starbucks, Bayer, and Japan's SMC.[39] The FDI allowed Costa Rica to move beyond balanced transactions to superior ones, resulting in additional investment and dramatic wealth creation. Wealth creation resulted because Costa Rica added capital coming from abroad to its existing local capital to increase business and economic activities, therefore exponentially increasing opportunities.

Qatar is another example of a country that used wealth acceleration tools to jumpstart its economy. Qatar recently experienced a blockade by some of its neighbors, which rocked the country's economy. Despite the sharp decline in some imports, Qatar's economy has rebounded over the last year or so.[40] One of the key areas of growth was in dairy production.

Before the blockade, Qatar had been heavily dependent on Saudi Arabia for 90 percent of its dairy products.[41] Baladna, one of the small businesses in Qatar that supplied dairy products, recognized the opportunity. In July 2017, Qatar Airways flew in 165 Holstein cows from Budapest, then added cows from Australia, the United States, Netherlands, and Germany. Baladna planned to have 14,000 cows by mid 2018.[42]

Baladna invested in livestock and machinery that allows it to produce 500 tons of fresh milk and yogurt daily, which meets domestic demand and allows surplus for export.[43] The country used to rely on imports from Saudi Arabia to meet that demand,[44] but thanks to several wealth acceleration tools, Qatar supplies its own daily products. The large farm is a tourist destination as well, with a zoo, park, and restaurant.[45]

Baladna planned an IPO in the first half of 2018 to raise funds for expansion.[46] This is just one wealth accelerator that Baladna is using. Instead of simply filling a portion of Qatar's need for dairy products using its current stock (balanced transaction), the company invested heavily in bringing additional cows and updating machinery to increase production and, therefore, wealth (superior transaction). Many accelerators were no doubt involved: capital investment, lines of credit, leverage, value chain, machinery, technology, natural resources, and so on.

Other superior transactions include turning its farm into a tourist destination. Instead of simply allowing people to visit, Baladna now welcomes them with a zoo, restaurant, tours, and a park. Just one of these would have sufficed, but adding additional business points allows Baladna to do more transactions than before, and all are superior transactions. Take a look at its state-of-the-art website—not to mention its technologically advanced machinery—and you'll see how Baladna has used technology as a wealth accelerator. Politics and the blockade aside, Baladna increased its superior transactions and its wealth, and supplied its country with much-needed dairy products.

Bangladesh has emerged as an unexpected success story, with the country once in ruins due to poverty and famine now outpacing neighboring Pakistan's GDP growth by roughly 2.5 percent.[47]

This transformation has many wealth accelerating factors, including social changes that began with the empowerment of women, government support of grassroots lending initiatives, and its successful garment manufacturing infrastructure. Labor laws allow large garment firms, thus allowing large economies of scale: lots of workers creating lots of garments, leading to lots of profit.[48] While additional appropriate regulation is needed to protect workers, Bangladesh's wealth accelerators of a large labor pool, positive government policy, and manufacturing infrastructure have created superior transactions where none existed before.

The city of Franklin, Tennessee, in the southern United States, has tapped into its cultural resources as a wealth accelerator. One of the bloodiest battles of the Civil War was fought on Carnton Plantation. Called the Battle of Franklin, wounded Confederate soldiers were brought to Carnton Plantation and Confederate dead were buried in the McGavock Confederate Cemetery on Carnton's grounds.

The venerable plantation, built in 1826 by Randal McGavock, finally left the McGavock family in 1911. It suffered years of neglect until 1977, when the house and ten acres were donated to the Carnton Association, Inc.[49] The association began restoring the home and grounds, which is today a popular tourist destination and an important stop for Civil War buffs.

Carnton Plantation now boasts an elaborate battlefield walking tour, the cemetery, guided tours through the plantation, a well-stocked gift shop and small museum, and hosts weddings and other events. The Carnton Association turned a neglected plantation into a series of superior transactions.

One wealth accelerator was the cultural significance of the historic site—the November 30, 1864, battle is believed to include the bloodiest hours of the war, with 7,000 Confederate troops killed or wounded. The cemetery also became the stuff of legend, with Carrie McGavock and her husband insisting upon digging up remains left on the battlefield and relocating them to the cemetery. She sent letters to the families of the dead, and is said to have walked in the cemetery until her death.

A balanced transaction might have been to restore the plantation house and offer tours. A superior transaction became tours, enhanced grounds and gardens, and a gift shop offering books related to the plantation and the Civil War. More superior transactions occur when the meeting room hosts weddings, and when tourists visit historic downtown Franklin and spend their money at restaurants and shops.

SUMMARY

The journey from trade to self-sustainability is one of small and large steps that start with a clear vision for what a country can become. That clear vision includes looking carefully at assets and liabilities and envisioning how each can be parlayed into superior transactions. Simply having an asset—such as the Grand Canyon or a large pool of cheap labor or technology infrastructure—doesn't create enough transactions to bring economic transformation. Basic transactions may result, but the move to superior transactions needs a push.

That push comes in the form of wealth creation accelerators, which allow businesses and governments to transform assets into superior transactions using a variety of means. Wealth accelerators can boost job creation and bring improvements to the country and its citizens' lives, but accelerators don't do the work alone. Leaders must have the vision to see what can be, the will to make necessary changes, and the power and ability to do so. Sometimes it's using simple and authentic opportunities that require little investment but a clear vision; other times it's a huge investment by individuals, businesses, foreign investment, and government to turn a country around.

Developing countries must be proactive, using the best and most appropriate wealth accelerators to optimize their assets and liabilities. They must take lessons learned from other countries and contextualize and maximize them in their own situations. Only then—when superior transactions result—will a country's citizens be able to lead better lives.

3

DETAILING THE OBED STUDY: HYPOTHESES AND SURPRISES

We've looked at Opportunity-Based Economic Development and how developing countries can move from a trade-based economy to a self-sustaining economy. We've also looked at how a country's assets and even its liabilities can provide opportunities for not only balanced transactions but also superior transactions. Finally, we've examined the wealth acceleration tools countries and businesses can use to produce more superior transactions and thus faster economic growth.

Now let's dig deeper into the details of the study we conducted to test the principles of OBED. After writing *From Aid to Trade*, I had a book in hand but not the research to definitively back up my suppositions. *From Aid to Trade* outlined what OBED looked like in a conceptual way, but were there data and statistics to support what OBED purported to do? The first book was based on interviews with in-the-trenches business people, those who run NGOs, tested business principles, and utilized deductive reasoning. We looked at how businesses normally grow and linked that growth to how countries grow. Multiply one business's growth by millions because the growth of a country is the sum of the growth of its businesses in economic value-added terms. Comparing business principles to a country's growth strategy is sound logically and valid in its application of the core principles of OBED.

The next step—deducing the cause and effect via a scientific and replicable model—is what we did through our research study and what we're showing in this book. By deepening OBED as a proven model that can be applied by developing countries, we can help their growth patterns and the people who live in those countries. But I first had to find a person who combined research and statistical analysis skills.

I met Egbert Kinds, a consultant who had done training for the NGO Parole et Action in Haiti. He and I had dinner on Curacao, a Dutch Caribbean island, where he was working at the time. As I told him about what I wanted to do, he immediately suggested Tim Smith, a Dutch researcher just out of university who was hungry to change the world. This would be his first big project. Our little team also included several senior advisers from the academic world at universities in both the United States and the Netherlands, who answered questions and offered input free of charge, which helped financially. Since I was financing the study myself, we couldn't spend an extended amount of time on the study. As with just about anything, the longer it took, the more expensive it became.

Tim's and my first emails were exchanged in August 2016 and we worked together for over a year, talking each Tuesday morning at 6 a.m. Haitian time, noon in the Netherlands. The conversations usually started with, "Hey, Tim, let me go get some coffee." We emailed regularly throughout the process, which had its fair share of ups and downs.

"The conceptual OBED model as presented in the first book is abstract," Tim said. "We needed to bridge the gap between concept and real-world measurables. Daniel is a very good conceptual thinker and very strategic, yet we needed to make his model measurable and replicable."

Tim was looking for clarity from me on direction and precision, but I was struggling with how to get concrete evidence from the cement, sand, gravel, and water of my abstract principles.

The main goal of the research was to translate the conceptual OBED model into an economic model that could be quantitatively tested. Our work began with describing the main economic relations the OBED model presupposes, then defining those relations using quantifiable economic variables. Lastly, we used the variable to run a regression of the model to verify whether real world data supports the model. The estimation of this regression uses data from thirty-eight countries.

HOW WE CHOSE THE THIRTY-EIGHT COUNTRIES

We studied thirty-eight countries, which is 19 to 20 percent of the world's countries and a good representation. We would have liked to study Haiti, my own country, but there wasn't enough data available from the World Bank and other sources.

We created a series of criteria upon which we chose which countries to study during a twelve-year period from 1995–2007, thus avoiding the worldwide financial crisis of 2008. Each country shared the following characteristics:

- GDP per capita of less than $10,000 in 1995

- Population of at least 1 million

- No major conflicts/wars between 1995–2007 (Pettersson & Wallensteen, 2008)

- Less than 10 percent of total GDP in 1995 came from the rent of natural resources such as mineral and mining rights (Pettersson & Wallensteen, 2008)

Countries that didn't make the list didn't fit these criteria, and/ or we couldn't find consistent data to allow us to study them and draw conclusions about how they were optimizing their assets. Fortunately, we found and studied enough countries to provide the underlying lessons that give us the formula for the path forward.

The list of countries we studied included:

38 Countries in Our OBED Study

Argentina	India	Panama
Bangladesh	Indonesia	Peru
Bolivia	Jordan	Philippines
Botswana	Kenya	Poland
Brazil	Latvia	Romania
Chile	Lithuania	Senegal
China	Malaysia	Slovak Republic
Costa Rica	Mauritius	South Africa
Croatia	Mexico	Thailand
Czech Republic	Moldova	Tunisia
Dominican Republic	Morocco	Turkey
Estonia	Namibia	Uruguay
Hungary	Nicaragua	

These thirty-eight were the countries for which the necessary data was available and that adhered to the constraints we set.

FIVE SECTORS OF THE ECONOMY

To translate the OBED strategy into an economic model, we divided the economy of each country into five different sectors: Agriculture, Forestry, Industry, Services, and Tourism. The five sectors mirrored those set up by the World Bank, and we used these five sectors because of the data available on them from the World Bank and other sources. The expectation was that countries whose economies followed the OBED strategy in these sectors on their paths to economic growth had higher growth than countries that didn't follow OBED strategies.

To research this we presumed that for every sector there is a critical underlying asset that is important to it. An asset is defined here as a resource with economic value that a country or individuals and corporations in a country own or control. The central presupposition is that economic development is most effective in sectors where assets and liabilities are already present, which is the case for all countries, not just those that are struggling. If this is so, then economic growth is best aligned with what is available in a country. Our study focuses on the alignment between available assets and sector growth, and presents a path that leads from available assets to transformation of those assets into superior transactions and wealth.

We developed two economic models by which we captured and applied the data and that showed the effects of OBED on the economy of a given country. The first is the Sector Level model, as shown below. We divided each country into five sectors, each with a corresponding asset and each with a corresponding variable by which we could measure:

Five Sectors of the Economy

	Sector	Asset	Variable
	Agriculture	Agricultural land	Percent of the total land area that is agricultural land
	Forestry	Forest land	Percent of the total land area that is forest area

	Industry	Cheap labor	Percent of the population that is unschooled
	Services	High-skilled labor	Mean years of education per capita
	Tourism	Cultural and natural history	Measure of cultural and natural beauty

We expected the revenue growth of each sector to be positively influenced by the sector's asset, with bigger and more usable assets resulting in stronger growth.

OUR TWO HYPOTHESES

As we conducted our study, we presumed two relationships. The first is a direct relationship between asset strength and growth in the sector which it supports. We expected that the more a critical asset is available in a country, the larger will be the growth in the sector it supports. For example, if a country has a larger pool of cheap labor this will positively affect growth in the Industry sector, for which cheap labor is a necessary input. Thus, our *Hypothesis 1*: *A strong underlying asset has a positive effect on growth in the sector it supports.*

The second relationship is between overall economic growth and the alignment of sector growth and asset strength. If growth is focused in the sectors where a country has the strongest critical assets, this alignment has a positive effect on overall economic growth. For example, if a country has a relatively large pool of cheap labor, growth of the Industry sector has a bigger long-term impact on economic growth than when the Industry sector grows in a country with a relatively small pool of unschooled labor.

Important here is that an asset only becomes valuable for economic growth when it is transformed into economic opportunity. The asset in itself is not expected to create economic growth. However, when there is growth in the sector it supports, the asset becomes effective. This led to *Hypothesis 2: Alignment of sector growth and assets has a positive effect on economic growth.*

TWO MODELS

To support our hypotheses, we developed two models: sectoral and national. On the sectoral level we expected the revenue growth of a sector to be positively influenced by the underlying critical sector asset, leading to the following model:

Model 1: Sector Level

$$G_{si} = a + \beta A_{si} + \varepsilon$$

(1) Where Gsi is the growth in sector s in country i, a is a constant and Asi is the extent to which the critical asset for sector s is present in country i. The error in the model is captured by E. The variable Asi is expected to be positive, because the more a critical asset is present in the country, the stronger growth is expected to be.

On the national level all five sectors are taken into account. The independent variable is the growth in gross domestic product (GDP) per capita. For every sector there are three independent variables: one that captures the asset, one that captures the strength of the growth in the sector that belongs to that asset, and a third variable that captures the interaction between the critical asset strength and the sector growth.

Model 2: National Level

$$Y = a + \beta A_{si} + \beta G_{sit} + \beta A_{si} \cdot G_{sit} + \varepsilon$$

(2) Where Yi captures the annual percent growth in GDP per capita in country i, a is a constant, Ais captures the strength of the critical asset for sector s in country i, $Gsit$ captures the relative growth of the revenue of sector s in country i in year t and $Asi*Gsit$ captures the interaction between Ais and $Gsit$. The error in the model is captured by E. The interaction $Asi*Gsit$ captures the positive effect of alignment between assets and relative sector growth.

This is the variable that measures the main OBED effect, because when it's positive it means there is extra growth in GDP per capita if Asi and $Gsit$ are high for the same sector. In model (2) the variables are written out for one sector s. For the complete model there will be three independent variables, and for every sector as well, leading to the following model.

$$Y_i = a + \beta AA_i + \beta FA_i + \beta IA_i + \beta SA_i + \beta TA_i + \beta GA_{it} + \beta GF_{it} + \beta GI_i + \beta GS_i + \beta GT_i$$

$$+ (\beta A_i \cdot GA_{it}) + (\beta F_i \cdot GF_{it}) + (\beta I_i \cdot GI_{it}) + (\beta S_i \cdot GS_{it}) + (\beta T_i \cdot GT_{it}) + \varepsilon$$

(3) *Ai* represents the Agricultural sector in country i at time t, *Fit* represents the Forestry sector in country i at time t, *Iit* represents the Industry sector in country i at time t, *Sit* represents the services in country i at time t, and *Tit* represents the Tourism sector in country i at time t. Interaction effects capture the alignment effect, which we call the OBED effect. We expect the coefficients for the interaction effects to be positive.

FIRST RESULTS

Our first regression ranked each sector simply on the presence of assets alone, presupposing, we hoped, the relationship between the presence of an asset and the growth in the sector it supports. For example, the presence of large tracts of agricultural land should reflect growth in the Agriculture sector; the presence of lots of cheap labor should reflect growth in the Industry sector.

But the formula didn't show this using data from the World Bank and other sources reflecting growth in those sectors for those countries. I was disappointed and wondered why our work had not yielded results. Was OBED skewed or wrong? Some are tempted to mold research to say what they want it to say, but I wanted credible research that supported the principles of OBED that I knew to be valid. How to find it?

We soon discovered the answer. We replaced the ranking method we originally used with the dummy method. Each asset needed a variable that we could test using data supplied by our sources. There were two main challenges in creating variables for assets. One was that the variable must capture the essence of the asset in a valid way. The second was that the variables must be comparable between countries. Because we wanted to compare the strength of sectors between countries, for every asset we constructed the variable as percentages of the total population, in per capita terms or in terms of a comparable scale.

For the Agriculture asset, we used data on the percentage of the total land area that is agricultural land based on information from the World Bank. Since this data is relative to the size of the country, it makes it possible to compare a large country like India with a small country like Latvia. We followed the same procedure for Forestry, where we used the percentage of the total land that is forest area.

The asset for the Industry sector is cheap labor. Here we used the percentage of the population that is unschooled, as an indication of the size of the pool of cheap labor compared to the total economy. Since this is a percentage of the total population, this statistic is comparable between countries. The asset for the Manufacturing sector is the same as for the overall Industry sector.

The asset for the Services sector is the high-skilled labor present in the country. Here we used education as an indication of skill level, using data on the mean years of education per capita.

Finally, for the Tourism sector we used data that ranks countries on a scale from 1–7 on the amount of natural and cultural beauty. The data was taken from The Travel & Tourism Competitiveness Report, 2015; we submit that the factors, such as UNESCO World Heritage sites and national parks that were used to create this scale, are relatively stable over time.

We created a new statistical equation to add in the variable, and began giving a 1 or a 0 to countries based on that variable. The top nineteen countries with the highest score on an asset were scored as a "strong asset;" the bottom nineteen countries received a "weak asset" score. Using the dummy variable, this meant a 1 or a 0. This formula allowed us to look at the relationships between multiple variables, to take real-world data and see how it correlates. The core of what we tried to do is see what empirical data was out there to back up my OBED presuppositions, and use science to support the conclusions.

We needed to adjust our approach a couple of times due to data constraints.

"The dummy idea was the key to successful research," he said. "We wanted to compare different countries, but also compare different sectors. It's difficult to compare unless you standardize, and to standardize we used the dummy variables."

GENERAL TRENDS

We discovered several general trends in the data. (See Appendix 1 for further details.) First is that the average annual GDP per capita in the thirty-eight countries increased 55.73 percent from 1995 to 2007. It started at 4694.95 in 1995 and grew to 7365.89 in 2007.

The biggest growth was seen in China (184.13 percent) and in the Eastern European countries of Latvia (164.77 percent), Lithuania (142.90 percent) and Estonia (141.01 percent). The slowest growth income per capita was in Kenya (11.18 percent).

Also, the share of the different sectors in total GDP changed in the twelve-year period. On average, the share of the Agricultural sector declined 4.35 percent; the share of the Forestry sector declined .52 percent; and the share of the Industry sector declined slightly at 0.20 percent. The Manufacturing subset of the Industry sector declined by 1.8 percent.

The most growth was seen in the Services sector share, up 4.25 percent. The Tourism sector also increased at 0.88 percent. These changes are in line with the general view that the weight of the world economy shifted away from Agriculture to, first, the Industry sector and now, more and more, to the Service sector.

SURPRISING RESULTS

Several things surprised us as we gathered, tested, and collated the data. First was the negative effect of large agricultural assets—land—on Agriculture sector growth. It seemed like lots of arable land should help sector growth. But the more agricultural land, the smaller the growth. This was not an intuitive finding, but a good finding to discover because it allowed us to intuit that developing the Agriculture sector—planting more crops on more land—probably isn't the best choice for growth.

Forestry reflected a similar pattern, with growth in the sector quite small. Having a lot of forest land didn't seem to be an advantage that leads to growth in the sector. For the Industry sector, the model captures the effect of having stronger Industry assets (a relatively high percentage of the population with no formal education) on GDP growth in the Manufacturing sub-sector. We expected a positive effect. The coefficient for the Industry assets is positive (0.31) and is significant. This indicates that countries with a larger pool of unschooled labor have indeed managed to turn this into opportunities. Countries with a large percentage of the population with no formal education have a .31 percent higher growth in GDP per capita in the Industry sector. If we use data on the Manufacturing sector instead of the broader Industry sector, the effects remain stable.

The fourth sector is Services. The model captures the effect of having stronger assets (a higher number of average total years of education) on GDP growth in the Services sector. We expected a positive effect. The coefficient for the Services sector is positive (0.26) but not significant, meaning that the results might be due to Services activity such as building hotels, theme parks, and cultural venues being counted in the Manufacturing sector.

The final sector is Tourism. Here the model captures the effect of having stronger tourism assets (a relatively high amount of natural and cultural beauty) on GDP growth in the Tourism sector. We expected a positive effect. The coefficient for the services sector is positive (0.08) but not significant.

Another surprise was the lack of results for the Tourism sector. Since this is such an important and relatively high-value service in many countries, I strongly expected more positive data. The more developed the Tourism sector is, the more growth in that sector, right? Yet growth was small. This required a little deduction on our part. Perhaps Tourism growth spilled over into Manufacturing or Industry growth, as building of hotels, resorts, restaurants, and roads would be counted under sectors other than Tourism. Perhaps the Services sector reaped the rewards of the huge food service and transportation needs required to undergird tourism. This phenomenon requires additional study, but suffice it to say that the Tourism sector didn't grow as much as I thought despite significant Tourism assets.

One more surprise was that the asset for the Industry sector, the presence of large numbers of unskilled laborers, didn't result in high positive growth in the sector. In fact, the presence of more high-skilled workers resulted in much more growth in the Services sector. This was an ah-ha moment for me because it confirmed the popular belief among economic experts that just having a lot of cheap labor doesn't help the purchasing power of individuals. Those cheap laborers can work all day earning less than the bare minimum that allows them only to survive, not thrive.

However, when we add a combination of cheap labor *and* highly skilled labor to a country's asset list, particularly in the Manufacturing (part of Industry) sector, we found a strong positive correlation of growth in that sector. This suggests that developed countries have a balanced mix of well-educated workers and lower-skilled labor that boosts growth in the Manufacturing sector. This has become a key principle in this book; readers will learn more about how the developing world can learn from this growth pattern in the next chapters.

EVIDENCE FOR OUR HYPOTHESES

We found evidence for both hypotheses in our research (*Hypothesis 1: A strong underlying asset has a positive effect on growth in the sector it supports* and *Hypothesis 2: Alignment of sector growth and assets has a positive effect on economic growth*). To test the first hypothesis, we ran a regression of the sector asset on relative sector growth. There was significant evidence of a direct effect for one sector, Industry. This means that countries with a lower-skilled labor force had more growth in their Industry sector. This effect remained stable if we only looked at the Manufacturing part of the Industry sector.

For the Forestry, Services, and Tourism sectors we found no evidence that the presence of useful assets has helped growth. For the Agriculture sector there was a significant negative effect. This means that in countries with higher amounts of agricultural land, there was a stronger decline in the importance of agriculture to the economy. This runs contrary to our hypothesis. Future research should take a closer look at this.

For the second hypothesis we ran a regression of asset strength, sector growth, and an interaction variable of asset strength and sector growth on overall GDP per capita growth. The interaction variable captures the alignment effect when there is high growth in a sector with a strong underlying asset. It gives the extra growth in GDP per capita that is caused by this alignment.

We found significant alignment effects for three sectors: Agriculture, Industry, and Services. There were no significant alignment effects for the Forestry and Tourism sectors. The results were the same whether GDP per capita or PPP per capita were used. First, the alignment effect for the Agriculture sector was positive and highly significant. This indicates that growth in the Agriculture sector has a stronger positive effect on GDP per capita in countries that have a larger amount of agricultural land.

Second, the alignment effect for the Industry sector was significant but negative. This means that the effect of Industry sector growth on GDP per capita is negatively influenced by a larger population of unschooled, cheap labor. This is interesting because earlier we found a direct positive effect of the presence of more unschooled cheap labor on Industry sector growth. These results seem to suggest that low-skilled labor helps growth in the Industry sector but hurts productivity growth.

We verified this by running a separate regression using an interaction between the Industry sector growth rate and an indication for high-skilled labor. The results showed a positive effect on GDP per capita growth by the interaction between Industry sector growth and a higher-educated labor force. This seems to suggest that higher-skilled labor increases GDP per capita in the sector. In other words, while a pool of low-skilled labor helps Industry growth, more education helps to increase the per capita money earned in the Industry sector.

Additionally, we ran a regression where we replaced the Industry sector with its sub-sector Manufacturing. Interestingly, the negative alignment effect disappeared. This indicates that a lower-skilled labor force does not negatively influence GDP per capita growth in the Manufacturing sector. This might be due to the fact that Manufacturing is a less high-skilled aspect of the Industry sector.

The third sector for which we found a positive significant alignment effect was the Services sector. This means that growth in the Services sector resulted in higher GDP per capita increases in countries with a higher-educated labor force.

Another result that should be discussed is the coefficients for the sector assets. None of the assets had a significant positive effect on GDP per capita growth. However, for the three largest sectors, Agriculture, Industry, and Services, there were significant alignment effects. This fits into OBED's view that assets in themselves do not help the economy. It's when they are being transformed into economic opportunity that they create value.

MORE RESULTS

The final results of the regression that should be discussed are the effects of sector growth on GDP per capita growth. Growth in the Agriculture sector and the Forestry sector had a significant negative effect on GDP per capita growth, while Industry sector growth had a significant positive effect on it. These results are in line with structural change that predicts that moving from lower productivity to higher productivity sectors is good for economic growth.

Contrary to expectations though, growth of the Service sector had a negative effect on economic growth. This may be something for future research to look into, especially since the alignment effect between the Services sector's high-skilled labor is positive and highly significant.

Overall, the results give credibility to OBED claims that assets play an important role in economic development. The interesting effects found in the Agriculture sector, the Industry sector, and the Service sector may prompt future research on this topic. The meaningful results also indicate that measurements of the assets for the three main sectors have validity. Since neither direct nor alignment effects were found in the Forestry and Tourism sector, future research might try to replicate this research with different asset measurements. Additionally, it would be interesting for policy makers to know whether there may be other assets that also play an important role in the Agriculture, Industry, and Service sectors.

A CHANGED PERSPECTIVE

For Tim, now working as a management trainee at DSM, a multinational Dutch chemical company, his perspective changed on developing countries. Aid, he said, isn't the complete answer. "This study made me think of developing countries more in terms of opportunities than in terms of problems. Simply giving countries money and/or food only addresses the problems in a country, not the opportunities," he said. "We must be careful that what we think are sound economic opportunities may be destroying economic growth."

My main hope is that developing countries continue to improve their institutions. This is where everything starts with regard to prosperity as a country. And I hope that these developing nations will take pride in what their assets can bring to the world. It's easy to feel inferior as a country; my hope and wish is that countries begin thinking of themselves in terms of strengths and opportunities.

This book's premise is that superior transactions bring about wealth and growth. Any country can move from aid to trade and from trade to self-sustainability using Opportunity-Based Economic Development strategies. The study described here is the foundation upon which growth is built.

THE FIVE PRINCIPLES OF GROWTH

We're now ready to dig deeper into the five principles of economic growth that undergird OBED, our research, and this book. The following five chapters will delve into one principle each to offer a thorough and careful look at what each one means for struggling countries eager to become self-sustaining. These principles are the bedrocks, the main lessons, of what our study shows.

The Five Principles of Growth

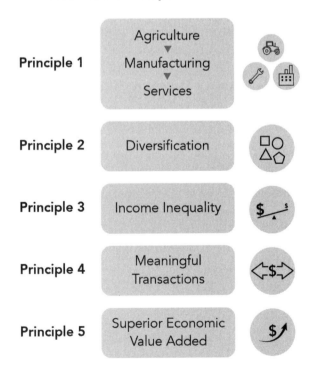

Principle 1	Agriculture ▼ Manufacturing ▼ Services
Principle 2	Diversification
Principle 3	Income Inequality
Principle 4	Meaningful Transactions
Principle 5	Superior Economic Value Added

Principle 1: In all the countries studied, growth and wealth accrued as countries moved first from an Agriculture-based economy to a Manufacturing-based economy, and then on to a Services-based economy. Developing countries need to imitate that pattern.

Principle 2: Developing countries should diversify in all sectors, investing in those sectors which promise the most growth while, in general, moving from Agriculture to creating more jobs in Manufacturing and Services.

Principle 3: Once countries move toward more jobs in the Services sector, income inequality is generated. When countries move from Manufacturing to Services, the underlying asset of cheap labor in one sector doesn't yield a higher income level in the other with those same workers.

Principle 4: Transactions are key to economic development. Focusing on meaningful, market-based transactions brings superior returns as businesses generate wealth, which creates more opportunities and more resources that create value for the business and society as a whole, without causing income inequality or other societal problems.

Principle 5: Simply having assets and (perceived) liabilities does not guarantee economic transformation. Without economic value added, those assets and liabilities must be transformed into meaningful transactions. Without that transformation, societies may end up being extremely poor and troubled despite possessing valuable assets.

4

THE PATTERN FOR GROWTH

Our study, designed to put OBED principles to the test with real-world, concrete facts, revealed a number of interesting patterns. Among them was that for countries to move forward economically they must move away from agriculture as a primary income source for both the country at large and its individual citizens—that is, at the sector *and* the national levels. This is stated as *Principle 1*: In all the countries studied, growth, wealth, and jobs accrued as countries moved shares of private investment, share of GDP and job creation first from an Agriculture-based economy to a Manufacturing-based economy, and then on to a Services-based economy. Developing countries need to imitate that pattern.

A study published by the Monthly Labor Review in 1984 says that in 1850, 64.5 percent of people in the United States were employed in the Agriculture sector, 17.7 percent in goods-producing, and 17.8 percent in Services. By 1984, the numbers were drastically different: 3.6 percent in Agriculture, 27.2 percent in goods-producing, and 69.2 percent in the Services sector.[50] Other developed countries around the world mirror that shift from primarily agrarian societies to societies based on jobs in the Manufacturing and Services sectors.

According to the World Bank, numbers of agricultural workers around the world dropped from roughly 43 percent in 1991 to just under 27 percent in 2017.[51] The opposite can be said for the Services sector. In 1991, almost 34 percent of jobs were in the Services sector; by 2017, that number was just about 51 percent.[52] Employment in the Industry sector, which includes Manufacturing, dipped slightly between 1991 and 2017, with several ups and downs in between. The 1991 percentage was just over 23 percent of the world's workers in Industry, while in 2017 that percentage was 22.5 percent.[53]

There are many things that influence these numbers—a country's political status, natural resources, levels of corruption, and natural disasters—but the trend I've seen through my study and reading the studies of others is that countries must move from Agriculture to Manufacturing (we are using this nomenclature interchangeably with Industry) to Services to find economic success. OBED principles can help countries make that change.

FOUR KEY WORDS

Four key words highlight the necessary action countries and leaders must take in this dynamic shift away from an Agriculture-based economy to, in the end, a Service-based economy. Developing countries must be *strategic* and *intentional* in *diversifying* shares of job creation and GDP growth from Agriculture to Manufacturing to Services, and must *specialize* in the areas in which they have competitive advantage within each sector, to create more superior transactions that create more growth faster.

Let's look at each word individually, then we'll look at what they mean together and look at several case studies of countries that have taken these steps.

First, *strategic*. Leaders must have a long-term strategy in place to make the move away from agriculture as the primary economic driver. This could mean creating or strengthening infrastructure such as ports, the electrical grid, technology grids, power plants, rail lines, and roads. It could also mean setting up an educational system that allows for learning opportunities that will feed the need for highly skilled workers in the future.

Being strategic also means setting aside funding, or creating new funding sources, to pay for this shift. Supporting factors such as those listed here must be in place to ensure the success of the transition from Agriculture to Manufacturing to Services. The better equipped a country is, the better the level of success; the less equipped, the less chance of success.

Second, *intentional*. Rather than simply reacting to changes in economic drivers, leaders are proactively moving ahead. This may mean creating laws to facilitate change, searching out Foreign Direct Investment opportunities, encouraging the banking industry to allow access to funding tools, educating the workforce, providing equal opportunities for women in the workforce, and so on.

Leaders must be forward thinkers to both inspire and assure entrepreneurs that the risks they take are worth it for themselves and the country, and that rewards will come. A country that isn't intentional goes nowhere fast. A country that looks forward equips itself with the ability to cope with adversities and challenges as they arise.

Third, *diversifying*. Agriculture isn't going away in a country; it's simply that fewer workers are needed as machines do more work. In fact, agricultural output has increased for decades in developed countries. What has decreased is the percentage of those employed in agriculture jobs and the percentage of GDP from the Agriculture sector. Manufacturing isn't going away either; it's simply that fewer workers are needed in low-skilled jobs as companies and countries move toward higher-skilled and higher-paying jobs producing higher-return goods in the Services sector. Again, it's not that the Manufacturing sector doesn't exist; it's that the percentages are diminished. A country hoping to improve must spread its workforce over all sectors, layering more heavily in the higher-return sectors such as Services.

Finally, *specialize*. Leaders and businesspeople must look at areas where they have competitive advantage and push hard in those areas, as these are the spheres where economic growth will happen through increased superior transactions. This doesn't mean that countries, businesses, and individuals embracing the path from Agriculture to Manufacturing to Services need to invest in every subsector, every business, and meet every need. They must focus on the areas that bring the best return on investment and most satisfaction to customers; they must focus on areas that are the most productive. This focus ensures that a country, by embracing this development pattern, does more superior transactions—rather than merely balanced transactions—as it moves forward.

KENYA MOVES AHEAD

Adan Mohamed is the Cabinet Secretary for Industry, Trade & Cooperatives for Kenya in East Africa. In a piece he wrote for Capital

Business in December 2017, he notes that massive investments in the energy sector and infrastructure (rail, roads, and airports), and expansion of the port of Mombasa led to remarkable progress in the ease of doing business. This in turn provided access to more markets (EU, AGOA, EAC), so that the stage has been set to take industrialization to the next level.[54]

The Naivasha industrial zone, located at the source of clean, green geothermal power, is one enhancer for large manufacturers;[55] another is a ten-year blueprint titled "Kenya's Industrial Transformation Program (2015–2025)," which identifies five key areas tied to existing advantages within the country, with ten particular opportunities to "increase manufacturing sector jobs to 435,000 additional jobs and at the same time add [Kenyan Shilling] (Kshs.) 200–300 billion to Kenya's GDP."[56]

Mohamed highlights several areas of specialization, including tea, coffee, and horticulture exports, leather processing, and textile and apparel manufacturing.[57] He also addresses possibilities in agro-processing, underlining that only 16 percent of exported agricultural products are processed. "Leveraging on processing opportunities could create an additional 110,000 jobs with Kshs. 60 billion in the offing for the economy," he said.[58]

Fish processing and providing construction materials that were once imported also can add to the growth of Kenya's economy, as can growth in IT, tourism, wholesale and retail markets, and growth of small and medium businesses. Progress has been made, said Mohamed, with Kenya now ranked 80th globally, up from 136th in 2013 in the World Bank Ease of Doing Business rankings.[59]

"From the onset, the pursuit of an inclusive model of growth that would provide millions of new jobs in the future has been embedded in the firm belief that the industrial sector through manufacturing would deliver the foundation for these jobs," says Mohamed. "The last four years have been about laying the foundation for creating a competitive manufacturing base both on infrastructure/cost front as well as on improving business environment. The time is now to put Manufacturing at the centre stage of Kenya's economic future."[60]

Kenya's leather sector has been a growth area for several years. With the Kenya Leather Development Council advocating on behalf of manufacturers, advising the government on matters relating to the sector, and advising investors, the sector promises even more growth.[61]

One example is the Kenya Leather Park being developed in Kinanie, Machakos County, near Nairobi. Ninety percent of Kenya's $94 million leather exports are unfinished. Leather experts and the government want to be processors of that leather and creators of leather goods, which will "create an additional 35,000 jobs and USD 150–250 million in GDP and contribute to substituting a portion of USD 86 million in shoe imports yearly."[62]

While the leather goods industry faces struggle such as smuggling, it plans to "have all hides and skins processed locally, set up 5,000 cottage industries, invest in four leather parks and support expansion of existing tanneries."[63]

Kenya is making a strategic effort to diversify its economy by moving away from Agriculture as its primary income provider of job and GDP growth and moving toward Manufacturing. While in no way doing away with its Agriculture sector and in fact moving toward growing its agri-processing businesses, Kenya is turning balanced transactions—farmer to distributor to exporter—into superior transactions by adding processing to the mix. Now the country can benefit from revenue and jobs created by agri-processing, plus still export those agricultural products.

It's also been intentional about building up trade in its specialty subsector of leather goods, creating infrastructure and government regulations to allow leather goods parks and attendant other businesses. While still on the road to a more Services-oriented economy, Kenya is well on its way up the ladder via its emphasis on Manufacturing.

Kenya is surrounded by countries still at the infancy stage of the OBED pattern of moving from Agriculture to Manufacturing to Services to increase economic growth. Kenya's leadership had the vision to move away from Agriculture, to veer away from its neighbors still dependent on the sector. Its move illustrates that it and countries such as Botswana, South Africa, Ethiopia, and Ghana understand the process of increasing agricultural production while decreasing workers in the sector, and of moving to manufacturing to creating more jobs and more wealth.

Let's look at a country in another part of the world.

THE EXAMPLE OF VIETNAM

Vietnam is an excellent example of a country that has made the move from Agriculture to Manufacturing and now into Services. It is well placed in Asia, surrounded by countries that have been better equipped for longer periods of time as they have made this move. Vietnam is surrounded by good examples of success, which provide it a better chance at success through better trade deals, trade blocs, and transfer of knowledge.

The study titled "Moving out of agriculture: structural change in Vietnam" by Brian McCaig of Wilfrid Laurier University and Nina Pavcnik of Dartmouth College was released in October 2013 and documents this development in Vietnam.[64]

Between 1986 and 2008, Vietnam's real GDP increased at an annual growth rate of 7 percent, with GDP per capita in PPP terms tripled; poverty rates fell. During this time of economic expansion, there was a huge shift in sector distribution. Agriculture started at 34 percent of GDP in 1986, and decreased steadily to 17 percent by 2009.

Manufacturing experienced growth, starting at 17 percent of GDP in 1986 and rising to 25 percent in 2009. And Services, which had the largest share of GDP, increased its share from 46 to 54 percent.[65]

Each sector's share of workers reflects this redistribution as well. In 1990, more than 70 percent of workers were in Agriculture, 18 percent in Services, and 8 percent in Manufacturing. By 2008, Agriculture was at 54 percent, Services at 32 percent, and Manufacturing up to 14 percent.[66] Another finding shows that Agriculture, with nearly 75 percent of employment, had the lowest labor productivity of all at less than one half of all productivity.[67]

What precipitated this change? Doi Moi, or "renovation," a series of reforms started in 1986 designed to help transform the economy by, in part, shifting labor out of Agriculture and into Manufacturing and Services.[68] Vietnam, with help from Doi Moi, made reforms throughout its system, mainly in agriculture, enterprises, and international integration.[69]

The Agriculture sector, which in 2009 was still the largest employer with 53 percent of workers, saw improvement in agricultural productivity that allowed workers to move into more economically productive sectors. What had once been organized through state-run collectives and experienced price controls, now moved into private enterprise that brought competition into the picture.[70]

Other reforms in the sector relaxed restrictions on trade of goods used in agriculture such as fertilizers, and rice export quotas were lifted. This was especially necessary because more than 75 percent of agricultural land was rice paddies. Between 1992 and 1997, rice export quotas rose from 1 to 4.5 million metric tons.[71]

Vietnam also reformed its restrictions on enterprises. Before Doi Moi, state-owned enterprises (SOEs) dominated production outside agriculture, producing nearly 30 percent of all output and half of output in Industry and Services, using about 16 percent of the labor force.[72] Doi Moi reforms allowed enterprises to make their own decisions regarding pricing, production, and trade. The government also began allowing foreign-owned businesses, offered tax incentives, exempted import and export duties, created economic zones, and allowed companies to form their own trading partnerships.[73]

Additional reforms included opening the country to foreign direct investment (FDI), leading to an influx of FDI and subsequent growth of output from FDI companies. The Enterprise Law also made it easier for companies to register, leading to 50,000 new enterprises in just under three years from January 2000 and October 2002. These reforms have made operating a business and making transactions infinitely easier in Vietnam.[74]

Another big step for Vietnam was becoming part of the global economy. Before Doi Moi, foreign trade was tightly controlled and exports were discouraged via controls and laws, not to mention a trade embargo imposed by the United States.[75] Other supporting factors were inflation control, reduction of the money supply, and a "basket" policy for price, wage, and monetary changes.[76] The country also created policies focused on creating a multi-sector commodity economy and opening the economy to competitive trade through foreign direct investment (FDI), official development assistance (ODA), and cooperation deals with countries in the region and around the world.[77]

Doi Moi also helped bring about greatly improved international relations. The country normalized relationships with the United States and nearly 170 other nations, and joined ASEAN (Association of Southeast Asian Nations).

According to a report by The Brenthurst Foundation titled *Manufacturing and Industry in Vietnam: Three Decades of Reform*, "In the reform period, Vietnam has signed over 90 bilateral trade agreements, nearly 60 agreements on investment incentives and protection, 54 agreements on double tax avoidance, and are currently developing trade relations with over 230 countries and territories. Vietnam has concluded eight Free Trade Agreements (FTAs)."[78]

Vietnam's leadership was intentional and strategic in its reforms affecting both domestic and international business. In doing so, it allowed diversification in products available for export. Exports shifted away from agricultural products such as rice and fish to manufactured products such as clothing, footwear, and office machines. Exports of crude petroleum also fell as Vietnam shifted from exporting primary products to exporting manufactured products made in the country.[79] This likely impacted the decline of the importance of the Agriculture sector and the increase of the Manufacturing and Services sectors as the country's emphases morphed. And as the sectors grew, so did the labor force needed to support them.

During the 2000s, employment in Manufacturing grew from 8 to 14 percent, with four main industries accounting for 61 percent of employment in the sector. Vietnam specialized in clothing, food products, beverages, furniture, and footwear.[80] While much can still be done in Vietnam, its move from Agriculture to Manufacturing/ Services has been a huge boon to a once-undeveloped country that is now becoming more prosperous.

OBED PRINCIPLES SUPPORTED

In our study of OBED principles in action, we captured the effect of having stronger agricultural assets (a relatively high percentage of the total land area that is agricultural) on sector revenue growth. We expected a positive effect, but the coefficient for the agricultural asset was negative and significant.

When we looked at the Agriculture sector relative to overall GDP per capita growth, we found a negative effect (–0.12). This is what we expected and is in line with structural change theory. We also looked at the effect of the interaction variables on GDP per capita growth. These interaction variables captured the main OBED effect, since they indicate the effect of the alignment between asset strength and relative sector growth on GDP per capita growth. Significant alignment effects between sector growth and asset strength were found for the three main sectors: Agriculture, Industry, and Services.

The alignment effect for the Industry sector is negative (–0.07) and significant at the 5 percent level. We expected that countries with a larger pool of unschooled workers would have more success in the Industry sector, which relies heavily on the presence of cheap labor. However, the relations seem to be more complex. While there was a direct positive effect from the presence of more unschooled cheap labor on Industry sector growth, the effect of Industry sector growth on GDP per capita is negatively influenced by a larger population of unschooled cheap workers.

To further investigate this relationship in the Industry sector, we ran an extra regression using an interaction between Industry growth and a variable that captures the amount of high-skilled labor in a country, rather than the size of the pool of unskilled labor. For this we used the asset for the Services sector (the mean years of education per capita). The coefficient for this alignment effect was positive (0.10) and significant at the 5 percent level. This indicates that while having a larger pool of unschooled cheap labor can be effectively used to grow the Industry sector, having higher educated people increases the per capita income that is earned in the Industry sector.

We also ran a regression where we replaced the Industry sector with its sub-sector Manufacturing. Interestingly, there is no negative alignment effect of the interaction between growth in the Manufacturing sector and the number of unschooled laborers on GDP per capita growth. This might be due to the fact that Manufacturing is a lower skilled sub-sector of the total Industry sector.

The third sector for which we found a positive significant alignment effect was the Services sector. This means that growth in the Services sector resulted in higher GDP per capita increases in countries with a higher-educated labor force.

These results are in line with structural change that predicts that moving from lower productivity to higher productivity sectors is good for economic growth. So, a developing country trying to generate economic growth as well as improve the lives of its citizens should look to move away from an agricultural-based economy first to a manufacturing-based economy, and from there move toward a service-based economy, a move consistent with popular and proven trends.

Underlying this data is the knowledge that simply making transactions—something individuals, businesses, and countries do every day—isn't enough. We can get by all day long making balanced transactions. It's making the move from balanced to superior transactions that can turn around a country, a business, and an individual's life.

When a country looks at its assets and liabilities, studies and makes decisions based on growth potential—such as moving from Agriculture to Manufacturing to Services—and begins moving toward superior transactions, wealth accrues and growth occurs.

DOMINICAN REPUBLIC, HAITI'S NEIGHBOR

The Dominican Republic shares the island of Hispaniola with Haiti (the island's native name is Quisqueya), and both countries share common histories until roughly 1960 when the two diverged. Since 1960 the Dominican Republic's GDP has increased by 5 percent a year and per capita GDP has quadrupled. GDP has increased by only 1 percent in Haiti, and per capita GDP has been halved.[81]

Productivity was "strongly negative" in Haiti from the 1960s to the 1990s, while it was generally positive in the DR. Most telling for our purposes is that during that time, 50 percent of Haiti's labor force worked in agriculture while only 18 percent of DR's labor force worked in agriculture.[82]

While relations between the countries have been for the most part strained, DR came to Haiti's aid after the devastating earthquake of 2010, which has opened some doors to perhaps a more cordial relationship.

In the area of global exports, DR "has achieved considerable product diversification and sophistication, while Haiti's exports have exhibited the opposite pattern." The DR has diversified its exports to include products "with relatively high technology content," while Haiti exports mostly primary goods or goods that require minimal processing.[83]

The 1980s were a time of growth for DR. By later in the decade, manufacturing was about 17 percent of GDP, employed about 8 percent of the workforce, and created about one third of exports.[84] Exports of manufactured goods went from 11 percent of exports in 1980 to a whopping 31 percent by 1987.[85] At the same time, Agriculture declined in importance. The 1960s saw nearly 60 percent of the workforce employed in agriculture, but by 1988 the sector employed only 35 percent of all workers.[86]

Dominican Republic, as of 2015, saw an annual growth rate of 7 percent; its Services sector, with emphasis on tourism, accounted for 65 percent of GDP. Industry (including Manufacturing) accounted for 32 percent of GDP, and Agriculture at 3 percent of GDP.[87] In fact, tourism increased 3.9 percent in 2017 with 6,187,542 tourists.[88]

How did DR move from Agriculture to Manufacturing to Services/ Tourism as the major economic driver? Like all developing countries do: through leadership, proactive decision making, diversification, and using economic accelerators to create growth.

DR eased restrictions to reduce the time needed to start a business and improved electrical and water services. The country also passed a law that made it quicker and less costly for commercial restructuring. The World Bank also helped the government finance rehabilitation of electrical lines to guarantee better service, two major dams, and 11,500 hectares of irrigated land to allow for better agricultural production.[89]

A key component of the increase in the Manufacturing sector has been Industrial Free Zones established throughout DR to encourage foreign business investment. In fact, DR has been ranked fourth in the world with respect to the number of Free Zone areas. Free Zones typically have lower or no import/export tariffs and taxes paid to the government, fewer rigid regulations, lower labor costs, and access to transportation and shipping facilities.[90]

The first Industrial Free Zone was established in 1969, with two more added by 1973 and companies within them totaling just over 100. The 1980s saw huge growth in Free Zones, FDI, and growth. Today there are 57 Industrial Free Zones around the country, with more than 500 companies finding a home in one of the zones. Telecommunications, textiles, footwear, assembly of medical and electronics components, and other industries thrive in these zones.[91]

Tourism is, of course, a huge Service sector boon to DR. The Caribbean Tourism Organization says almost 6 million visitors came to DR in 2017, a 6.7 percent increase from 2015. Tourism has increased from 1.8 million visitors in 1998; the government hopes to draw 10 million visitors annually by 2023.[92]

An increase in tourism means an increase in other sectors as well. Manufacturing grows as hotels spring up (DR expects approximately 18,000 new hotel rooms will open between 2016 and 2019[93]), as infrastructure is strengthened to accommodate more tourists, as restaurants open, as tourist attractions increase, and as food must be available to feed everyone. Workers are needed in these areas, yielding overall economic growth.

Thus, transactions are being enhanced through manufacturing and tourism. Dominican Republic has increased its share of superior transactions as its economy grows, which in turn yields more superior transactions. DR has taken steps to ensure that these transactions increase by opening the door to businesses through Free Zones and better infrastructure such as sea ports and airports; by increasing tourism through development of hotels, restaurants, beaches, and other tourism-related business, as well as better air travel and communications; and through an increase in telecommunications infrastructure to allow other Service industries—such as call centers and data centers—to thrive.

The country has increased agricultural output as its labor force in agriculture shrinks—one of the key principles of OBED—while growing in the Manufacturing and Services sectors.

THE NECESSITY OF AGRICULTURE

Let me say strongly here that Agriculture will never disappear as a viable sector in a country's economy. Farms are needed to produce food that feeds the country (and hopefully provide products for export). In fact, the number of agricultural products produced around the world has increased. Manufacturing will also always be part of a successful country's economic base as companies large and small produce products people use every day.

I want to emphasize that the portion of workers in those sectors decreases as technology allows for fewer workers needed, and as education levels increase, allowing more workers in better jobs such as those provided by the Services sector, which increases GDP per capita across the spectrum.

My homeland, Haiti, hasn't yet made the leap like the Dominican Republic has. In Haiti, you can see 50 people working the fields with hoes and pickaxes; in developed countries, it would be one person on a tractor. In developed countries such as the United States, Germany, France, and Canada, roughly 3 percent work in the Agriculture sector. In Haiti, that number is 50 to 70 percent, with Haiti no different from other undeveloped countries.

Haiti has a prime example of economic growth in its neighbor, Dominican Republic. DR's exports to Haiti have grown from 3 percent of all exports in 2000 to close to 15 percent in 2009, with DR supplying 30 percent of Haiti's imports.[94] The report suggests several changes that could help Haiti begin to move toward its more successful neighbor, among them promoting trade diversification by new firms of new products to new destinations; investing in infrastructure; and reducing transaction costs such as shipping and customs requirements.[95]

Let's move on to consider the next principle—that of diversifying in all sectors.

5

THE NEED FOR DIVERSIFICATION

Now let's take a look at *Principle 2:* Developing countries should diversify in all sectors, investing in those sectors which promise the most growth while, in general, moving from Agriculture to creating more jobs in Manufacturing and Services.

We talked a bit about diversification in the previous chapter, and now we want go deeper into what diversification means and looks like for developing countries. We know it doesn't mean focusing on only one sector—such as just Manufacturing or just Services—because it's not been proven through our OBED study, at least not yet, that countries can survive and thrive if stalled on one phase of the journey to success.

In fact, our study showed that the group of thirty-eight countries didn't stay focused on even two phases of the journey. The trend present in all of these countries showed that diversification in *all* sectors led to economic growth and stability. Our OBED premise is that if developing countries emulate this pattern, each one can find a way to provide higher economic return.

As countries make the move from Agriculture to Manufacturing to Services, they continue to invest in all of the sectors; the investment percentages, however, look different as countries move forward. Agriculture doesn't represent a large portion of investment for developed countries because it doesn't have to be—thanks to technology and better farming techniques. Also, these countries don't want Agriculture to be a large investment because GDP growth and wealth accumulate better and faster through Manufacturing and Services.

The United Kingdom's Agriculture contribution to its GDP is just 0.61 percent, the smallest of any nation in the world. Yet the sector produces 60 percent of the food needed for the nation while employing less than 2 percent of the labor force. The UK instead focuses on Services, particularly banking and insurance.[96] Other developed countries with low percentages of Agriculture contributions to GDP include Belgium at 0.74 percent, Germany at 0.75 percent, and Denmark at 1.27 percent.[97]

I recently spoke at a conference in the Netherlands, and after the conference several friends and I rented a car for a trip through the European countryside. We drove from the Netherlands to Germany to Belgium to France. I saw farmland everywhere, with crops growing in vast fields in every country. What I didn't see was people in those fields. If I saw anyone, it was one driver on one tractor. Clearly these countries were still investing in Agriculture; but technology and advancements in farming techniques had reduced the number of people needed to produce the same amount or even more food.

Countries with little arable land are also finding ways to use what they have for agriculture gains. Egypt, for example, which is 90 percent desert, is reclaiming some of the desert through irrigation systems to use as farmland; and Suriname, a tiny country on the northeastern coast of South America, has 12 percent of its labor force employed in agriculture, despite having the smallest percentage of land used for agriculture in the world.[98]

Countries shouldn't skip Agriculture, but instead leverage what they have to produce something that gives them the best edge. If you have any advantage in the Agriculture sector, use it no matter how small a percentage the sector is in GDP. That's what diversification is: finding a shred of opportunity and maximizing it across all sectors.

Countries thrive when they diversify their base and specialize in particular areas within the sectors that match their assets. It hasn't been proven through research that countries can completely skip one or two sectors and still thrive. A better plan is to strategically move investments, GDP growth, and job creation from the most expensive (costs more to do less) sectors to the least expensive (costs less to do more) ones, which brings a higher level of efficiency and effectiveness.

Let's look closer at how to find opportunities to diversify and specialize as countries move through the Agriculture–Manufacturing–Services journey. We'll look at how countries can invest in assets that will strengthen the sectors they want to focus on, and at assets that can strengthen already developed sectors. We'll also look at the accelerators countries can use to facilitate this journey. How wealth is created and its results are the same regardless of the sector: more superior transactions. Innovation and invention do the same things for Agriculture as they do for Manufacturing and Services: again, more superior transactions.

THE NETHERLANDS

The Netherlands explodes the myth that small countries can't tap into the Agriculture sector because of lack of arable land. This country of almost 42,000 square kilometers (roughly 16,000 square miles) is the world's top exporter of potatoes and onions despite its size. It is also the top producer in tons per square mile of chilis, green peppers, and cucumbers, and in the top five globally for pears and carrots.[99] The country is also a global leader in exporting tomatoes (a warm-weather fruit) and vegetable seeds.[100]

How can a small country be such a large exporter of agricultural products? Innovation, invention, research, and development. Huge greenhouse complexes dot the country, often located within sight of bustling cities. The climate-controlled farms allow crops to grow despite winter weather, rain, and seasonal changes.[101]

One of the key accelerators for the Netherlands rising to the top of food production is research done at Wageningen University & Research (WUR), which is widely seen as the top agricultural research institute in the world.[102] Plant Sciences and commercial and market research operate side by side at WUR to meet the challenge to, as plant sciences managing director Ernst van den Ende says, produce "more food in the next four decades than all farmers in history have harvested over the past 8,000 years" to meet food needs for the world's growing population.[103]

For the Dutch, that research means huge growth in the Agriculture sector as farmers implement the findings, producing much more with much less. The Duijvestijns' 36-acre greenhouse complex near Delft grows fifteen varieties of tomatoes on twenty-foot vines in an indoor environment heated thanks to geothermal aquifers flowing under much of the Netherlands.[104] Plants are rooted in a fiber-based mix instead of soil, which uses much less water than plants in open fields.[105] The Duijvestijns regularly attend meetings of farmers and researchers at WUR because, as Ted Duijvestign says, "No one knows all the answers on their own."[106]

Another Dutch farmer, Jacob van den Borne, uses drones to increase yield on his potato farm. Two drones, one a driverless tractor roaming the fields and the other a flying quadcopter, give him readings on water content, nutrients, and growth, down to the individual plant. Does it work? His fields produce more than twenty tons per acre while the global average is nine tons.[107]

The Dutch also lead the way in biological pest and disease control thanks to Koppert Biological Systems, started by Jan Koppert after he was diagnosed as allergic to the pesticides he sprayed on his cucumbers. Now the company employs 1,330 and has twenty-six international subsidiaries, and is happy to send you bags of ladybug larvae, bottles of predatory mites, boxes of nematodes, and boxes of visiting bees to pollinate flowers.[108]

Manufacturing is a large part of the Dutch economy as well. The Netherlands' tax structure supports industry; infrastructure in communications and distribution is well developed; and an educated, multilingual workforce contributes to the country's economic growth.[109] Industrial goods make up about a third of all Dutch exports, and the Manufacturing sector ranks third behind Germany and Austria in terms of growth.[110]

The Netherlands is home to multinational companies looking for a European base. Industrial giants such as Mars, Coca-Cola, Kraft Heinz, Eastman, Verizon, and Damen Shipyards have operations there.[111]

The Kraft Heinz Company opened its Center of Excellence in May 2018 in a business district in Amsterdam as part of its plan to make its Netherlands operations a "global growth engine."[112] Kraft Heinz is also opening a new Heinz Ketchup line at its Elst facility, to come online in 2019.[113] The Center of Excellence will focus on new methods for working smarter and with more efficiency in logistics and food production, among other things.[114] Heinz, the company that urged farmers in Holland, Michigan, to produce more cucumbers back in the 1890s (see chapter 2), continues its manufacturing now using advanced technology to make the same things it did then: pickles, ketchup, mustard, and a host of other products. The Dutch-based Damen Shipyards Group manufactures on a much larger scale, building vessels of all sizes and uses. The company was started by Jan and Rien Damen in 1922, expanding under the guidance of Kommer Damen, who bought the company from his father in 1969 and introduced the concept of modular construction, or standardization, to build smaller boats.[115] Now with a global workforce of more than 9,000, Damen produces up to 180 vessels a year.[116]

Damen, through the years, has acquired shipyards around the world and branched into ancillary businesses such as repair, conversions, and maintenance.[117] Damen started as a small boat-making business, used the technology available in the 1960s and 1970s to grow its manufacturing capabilities, and today continues that manufacturing using the latest technology and a global workforce. You can almost see the accelerators at work: research and development, loan packages, technology, sound infrastructure, pro-business laws, invention, and the list goes on.

Services contributes to the strong Dutch economy in vital ways. The Dutch banking and financial industries have a "well-developed financial infrastructure,"[118] and there is a large network of financial brokers plus an international focus in the industry.[119] Gross value inserted into the economy from the banking/financial sector was 5.5 percent in 2015, with employment at about 70,000 full-time equivalent in 2016.[120] Three large institutions—Rabobank, ING, and ABN Amro—control 60 to 80 percent of the market share.[121]

Dutch financial institutions are participating in, yet watching carefully, investment in financial technology (FinTech), a growing area in the Services sector.[122] FinTech includes mobile banking including payment transfers, iDeal, contactless payments, e-commerce service providers, crowdfunding platforms, asset management, financial advice, insurance initiatives, and individual bank initiatives. The drive behind FinTech is that such innovation reduces the cost of data collecting, storing, processing, and exchange.[123]

"Innovation is in principle beneficial to prosperity. It provides for better products and services, and increases competition, diversity, efficiency and transparency. Innovation is inherent to a sector that is exposed to market forces," says DeNederlandscheBank.[124] The Netherlands is a prime example of an economy that has diversified across the Agriculture, Manufacturing, and Services sectors, with all contributing to the GDP. Its vital Agriculture sector grows more food with less land; Manufacturing continues to streamline practices to increase productivity; and Service businesses undergird all of it.

Two of the best accelerators—as seen in the Netherlands, the UK, and other countries—across all sectors are innovation and invention. We've seen what invention (tractors, other farm equipment) and innovation (disease resistant seeds, better fertilizers) have done for the Agriculture sector. History shows us what innovation and invention have done for the Manufacturing sector (think Industrial Revolution and beyond), and we've seen what the dynamic duo have done in recent years in the Services sector (technology, information systems, AI).

AI—Artificial Intelligence, sometimes called Machine Intelligence—allows machines to do what humans once did. AI is revolutionizing sectors such as Manufacturing, as machines now make products that once took multiple employees. As computers have become better at storing and increasing computing power, machine intelligence has grown. It's beyond the scope of this book to delve into the intricacies and myriad applications of AI, but suffice it to say that manufacturing and all other sectors will never look the same again.

While AI can look scary—creepy robots taking over the world and robots replacing every manufacturing job the world over—what it really does is present opportunities. AI can allow businesses to make more products for less cost and with less error margin; AI can use algorithms to discern what buyers want and present your products to them; AI uses what is called "deep learning" to analyze data at high speed to allow companies to see trends and even flaws.

We see AI at work nearly every day via Siri and Alexa, self-driving cars, refrigerators that tell us what foods we're out of, and when we play chess with the app on our phones.

Lindsay Whitfield, of the Danish Institute for International Studies, conducted an extensive study on how countries can become rich and reduce poverty. She concludes, "It is not agriculture and

manufacturing per se that matter, rather the bundle of characteristics typically associated with these different economic activities
which embody the potential to create wealth or reduce it. Countries
become wealthy by specializing in economic activities which embody
increasing returns, technological change, and synergies with other
industries in the economy."[125]

When it comes to growing GDP and overall wealth, countries
don't have to skip a sector; they can maximize and amplify using
innovation and invention in every sector. For example, Iceland
and Switzerland have lots of ice and rocky areas so they don't put
emphasis on agriculture, yet they continue to maximize the sector.
Much of Switzerland's arable land (10 percent of total land area) is
used for raising cattle whose milk is used for cheese, yogurt, and
milk for chocolate, while the rest is used to grow cool weather crops
such as fodder, cereal grains, root vegetables such as potatoes and
sugar beets, and as vineyards.[126] Iceland, with only a fifth of its
land suitable for crops, devotes much of its arable land to raising
livestock; crops include cold-weather staples such as potatoes and
other root vegetables.[127]

Iceland and Switzerland are tapping into the resources they
have to add to the economy. Each one takes advantage of its cooler
weather and small amount of arable land to its best benefit—growing cool weather crops and raising livestock. That's what we're
talking about with a country's economy. Using resources at hand
and adding accelerators makes the country even more successful.
But undeveloped countries are lacking those crucial elements or
have neglected to use them to their fullest extent.

HAITI AND MANGOES

Haiti is one such country missing out on opportunities to boost its
economy by exporting goods and investing in value chain operations for those exports. Take mangoes and other organic fruits,
for instance. Haiti's Agriculture sector could be producing enough
mangoes to expand exports to the U.S. and European markets.[128]
Should Haiti decide to invest in mango production and export, it
could simply export the mangoes fresh from the trees. Or it could
invest in value chain operations such as processing and packaging
plants to harvest its own superior transactions. Instead of exporting
mangoes only, it could export packaged mango products.

According to Fresh Plaza, the demand for mangoes has grown 5 percent annually for the last decade, with 1.8 million tons traded annually.[129] Peru and Ecuador are big suppliers of mangoes, as are India, Brazil, Australia, China, the Philippines, and Vietnam (which just gained access to U.S. markets), among others.[130] Mango products include fresh mangoes and processed products including canned and frozen slices, dried mangoes, salsa, sorbet, candies, and juice.

Haiti—using financial accelerators such as FDI, loan products, and other tools to build mango processing and manufacturing plants—could be producing superior transactions thanks to value chain optimization. More Haitians could be employed in these plants, taxes could be collected from individuals and businesses, and all three sectors—Agriculture, Manufacturing, and Services—could benefit from expanding the mango value chain.

Haiti is leaving superior transactions on the table. By not maximizing and amplifying its assets—in this case mangoes—Haiti misses out on trading opportunities, ancillary business related to processing and exporting mangoes, and economic growth. Think several steps up the value chain: website design for the processing companies, service department jobs to answer business-related calls, human resources people to hire production workers, and marketing experts to "sell" Haitian mangoes to potential importers. The value chain continues to expand as businesses expand.

This scenario begs another question: should Haiti focus solely on the Agriculture sector because it can grow mangoes? Not according to OBED strategy, and neither should other developing countries. The key is to diversify assets throughout Agriculture, Manufacturing, and Services to create a balanced economy. Should Haiti focus on mango growth within Agriculture? Yes, if that specification makes sense because of land and climate perfect for growing mangoes, manufacturing plants that can process them, and easy access to shipping routes to export them, particularly because the biggest market and economy in the world—the United States—is less than a one-hour plane ride away.

Developing countries should find the things they are good at, or at least better at, and focus on those as these countries look to move from Agriculture to Manufacturing to Services and look to diversify and specialize within those sectors.

IVORY COAST AND COCOA BEANS

Ivory Coast, long a grower of cocoa beans, has been hurt by its inability to process those cocoa beans. Instead, Ivory Coast would export most of the beans to another country, which would process them and gain the economic benefit of building the processing plants, higher employment, taxes, etc. Now Ivory Coast is working toward processing those cocoa beans itself.

A recent Reuters news article cites "fiscal measures and incentives given to companies" as accelerators that plan to increase the cocoa bean value chain. Companies receiving the incentives will invest that money into additional bean-grinding apparatus to increase capacity by 7.5 percent for each company by 2022, according to the article.[131]

"According to Ivorian cocoa grinders, energy costs, the cost of importing machinery, and getting qualified plant maintenance specialists, are factors that make local grinding less attractive compared with options outside Ivory Coast," the article says.

Hence the government has provided accelerators to keep cocoa bean grinding in-country. Even with the incentives and if goals are met, Ivory Coast would still grind only 50 percent of its cocoa beans.[132] After more than a decade of civil war that ended in 2011, the country experienced an influx of foreign investment and economic growth; in fact, Ivory Coast's growth rate has been among the world's highest.[133]

Agriculture engages the majority of the population—roughly two thirds, according to the World Factbook—and the GDP per capita and PPP has grown from $3,500 in 2015 to $3,900 in 2017.[134] Yet how much more growth could occur if Ivory Coast expanded its value chain regarding cocoa beans. The Manufacturing sector would grow as more plants are built to accommodate specificity in processing cocoa beans; the Services sector could grow as technology and communications needs expand for manufacturers and ancillary businesses associated with exporting the beans. Taxes could be collected, infrastructure strengthened, and a portion of the 46.3 percent of people living below the poverty line might begin to see a better life.[135]

Ivory Coast is certainly engaging in sectors outside of Agriculture. Industries include wood products, oil refining, gold mining, textiles, fertilizer, building materials, and electricity, among other things.[136] It's no surprise for anyone studying OBED principles that Agriculture makes up 17.4 percent of GDP in Ivory Coast; Industry at 28.8 percent; and Services at 53.8 percent.[137]

While Ivory Coast is beginning to diversify sector allotment with regard to cocoa beans, the country is still leaving many superior transactions on the table. Its Agriculture sector is held hostage to the whims of the international market regarding cocoa bean exports, while its Manufacturing sector is missing out on factories to clean, grind, package, and send those beans. Superior transactions are being missed.

Let's look at Ivory Coast's cocoa bean industry from several perspectives to see how it's improving but also to see what needs to improve. The Cocoa Life website offers a story about one farmer, Amadou Ouattara, who is a member of ECAM, a cooperative of more than 900 farmers in Ivory Coast's Cocoa Life program.

He is a third-generation cocoa farmer, and father to eleven children. Ouattara has struggled with worn-out soil, access to seeds and seedlings for new plants, and not enough access to fertilizers and compost to augment the soil. Cocoa Life offered training to its member farmers, allowing Ouattara to learn about pruning his trees for better yield and fighting disease.

"Before joining the Cocoa Life program, I was producing 350 kilograms of cocoa per hectare. Today, after two and a half years in the program, my yield has almost doubled, to 600 kilos per hectare," said Ouattara.[138]

Accelerators: Joining Cocoa Life, knowledge gains, accessing fertilizers, increased yield.

Olam International, based in Singapore, built a new cocoa processing plant in Abidjan in Ivory Coast that became operational in 2012. Olam invested $43.5 million in the plant that complements Olam's other cocoa business in the country to "develop an integrated cocoa supply chain."[139] Olam knows that processed cocoa beans result in higher profits, and that there are advantages to distributing cocoa products instead of just cocoa beans to the worldwide chocolate market.[140]

The new plant processes 60,000 megatons (Mt) of cocoa beans, creating cocoa liquor and cocoa butter for the chocolate industry, and cocoa cake that is made into cocoa powder, which is exported to Spain where it is distributed by Olam's milling plant.[141]

Olam partners with a multinational chocolate company as a supplier, and has helped train farmers in best practices for growing the best beans. It has given improved seeds to farmers, built solar dryers to dry the cocoa beans, and provided incentives to farmers to improve the quality of beans they provide.[142] Ivory Coast was chosen because of a "favorable economic environment," access to high-quality beans, good export policies, and strong infrastructure.[143]

Accelerators: Investment from parent company, vision for cocoa products, training and supplying farmers, good economic environment, favorable export policies, good infrastructure.

Ivory Coast's cocoa beans have prompted growth in the Services sector thanks to entrepreneurs taking advantage of resources close to home. Dana Mroueh is a chocolatier who uses beans grown in Ivory Coast for her Mon Choco chocolate. Unfortunately, despite growth in cocoa bean value chain, very little chocolate is made in Ivory Coast.[144]

Mroueh buys the beans directly from farmers, dries them on the roof of her factory or in a tumble dryer, then grinds the crushed beans, with brown sugar also made in Ivory Coast, in a machine attached to her bicycle. After days of grinding, a dark paste forms which is put in molds and chilled.[145] Mrough sells her chocolate directly to consumers. This entrepreneur combines simple manufacturing—making the chocolate herself—and relatively simple Service sector work—website, POS technology, advertising, human resources—as she sells chocolate directly to consumers.

Retailers are just one aspect of the Services sector that could be, and to some extent is, utilized in Ivory Coast with regard to cocoa beans. However, like other developing countries, Ivory Coast is lacking people to work in the Services sector. Several factors may contribute, including lack of an education infrastructure to provide necessary training, talent drain as educated people leave the country for a better life elsewhere, and lack of high-paying jobs in the sector.

Think about what could happen on a large scale if Ivory Coast invested in Service sector jobs. In relation to the cocoa bean sector of the economy, Service jobs could include banking, manufacturing, website creation and services, data analysis, human resources, advertising, education, and transportation services.

All of this is going on in Ivory Coast on a small scale. Some balanced transactions are taking place. But think about the possibilities of large-scale Service sector growth on GDP, PPP, and the everyday life of its citizens. By searching along the value chain from cocoa bean growing to the end products, Ivory Coast can add wealth and make superior transactions in all sectors.

Economist Kady Fadika Coulibaly says, "We are not keeping for the population the bulk of the added value that could be taken from agriculture. We need to transform [the cocoa] to be able to have more employment for the people who are working now on the plantations [so] they can also be working in the factories."[146] I would add, "and in the Service sector too."

TECHNOLOGY IS KEY

One of the key ways a country moves into the Service sector is through technology. We've seen its uses in all areas of the economy and our lives. In Ivory Coast, cell phone subscriptions rose from .47 million in 2000 to 27.45 million in 2016.[147] In Haiti, cell phone subscriptions went from .64 per 100 inhabitants in 2000 to 60.54 in 2016.[148] In the U.S., 95 percent of adults use a cell phone of some kind, while 77 percent use a smartphone.[149] Cell phones are just one of many enabling technologies allowing the Service sector, as well as other sectors, to grow. Cell phones allows superior transactions to occur such as mobile banking and data sharing, social media to exist, connect people and businesses, and do more business at multiple levels. Cell phones allow accelerators to magnify their impact via these small devices.

There are uncountable uses for technology as accelerators in business. The bookselling industry has been hit hard by technological innovation in the form of Amazon, with the Christian bookselling industry particularly troubled. Amazon siphons off a big percentage of shoppers who would normally have visited bricks-and-mortar stores to purchase books and gifts, which has a big impact on the smaller "Christian" demographic. Small mom-and-pop stores have been closing left and right, and the large chain Family Christian closed nearly 350 stores around the country in

2017. Lifeway announced in early 2019 that it would close its 170 bricks-and-mortar stores as well.

How can Christian stores stay open? In part by learning about its customer base through POS data gathering, gathering date via website hits and usage, and studying sales numbers. And by offering those customers what they want based on that knowledge. Baker Book House, an independent Christian store in Grand Rapids, Michigan, learned its customers wanted more places to gather, so the store increased seating and made sure there were outlets to plug in computers and cell phones. Customers want coffee, tea, and light snacks so the store added a café. The store also grew its children's area, offered more and varied events at the store, deepened its gift line, and provided a community meeting room.

The goal is to learn what customers want and provide it for them, plus bring new customers into the stores. Imagine all stores doing this; it could boost the entire industry. Christian retailing is a small segment of the overall retail industry. Imagine the impact of specific knowledge (an accelerator) about specific consumers.

Ann Byle, who contributed to this book, sees the results in her mailbox. She shops at Grand Rapids, Michigan-based Meijer stores for groceries. About every two weeks she receives a small mailer of eight coupons for products she buys at almost every visit: Meijer milk, Oreo cookies, Snack-Pak pudding, Pillsbury rolls, and green grapes. Occasionally, after purchasing something off the usual list such as cat treats or tea, she receives a coupon for those items. A little disconcerting? Yes. Reality? Yes.

Data is king, and companies using data to learn who their customers are and what they want are gaining sales and gaining wealth. Data gathering and use is just one way technology is used as an accelerator. Technology as an accelerator is also ubiquitous in medicine and healthcare; music production and distribution; the banking and financial sectors; and almost every other sector in the economy.

Yet technology is useless if there is no or limited physical infra-structure to support it, which is where developing countries fall short. Ann and I are constantly hampered by a poor internet connec-tion in Haiti as we work on this book via phone calls, Skype calls, and Google Docs. A high-tech business can make all the products it wants, but if there are bad roads, washed-out bridges, and no ports to ship from, the product sits in a warehouse.

CONCLUSION

Several important takeaways from this chapter rise to the surface in this look at how developing countries can move from poverty to wealth. First is that the move from dependence on the Agriculture sector for jobs and wealth creation to the Manufacturing sector and then to the Services sector is a tried and true path out of poverty to wealth. Agriculture has the lowest returns for the highest level of labor, while Services has the highest return for the least effort. For instance, in times past a large percentage of the population worked in agriculture, yet agriculture's contribution to the GDP was lowest of all three sectors. Countries that adjust their investment in regard to GDP and job creation remain competitive in the Agriculture sector. Those that focus resources in the Services sector—technology, financial systems, and insurance systems, to name a few—create more wealth faster and improve the lives of many more of its citizens.

The second takeaway is that countries should put effort into all three sectors instead of eliminating one or two altogether. Research shows that investment in all sectors is important; more important is the percentages of each sector. As a developing country moves from poverty to wealth, the scales tip from heavy investment in Agriculture to heavy investment in Services.

The Netherlands still focuses pointedly on Agriculture and is innovative in the field, yet continues to develop its Manufacturing and Services sectors through technology, innovation, and invention. This trajectory of work in all sectors to use each to its best advantage has countries heading toward better economies.

The third takeaway is to find what a country or region excels at and focus energy there in all sectors. Ivory Coast is good at growing cocoa beans; it shouldn't stop growing cocoa beans just because the Agriculture sector is high-effort/low-return as far as GDP is concerned. Instead, it should use that cocoa bean asset and magnify it into growth in the Manufacturing and Services sectors. Using accelerators to boost sector growth is vital to an improved economy.

The fourth takeaway is that technology changes everything. All sectors and all specialties can benefit in some way from technology, whether through drones to check on crops or through behind-the-scenes data analysis. Developing countries do well to invest in infrastructure that pushes technology forward such as wireless communications, technology education, and computer services.

Countries that avoid or can't make the move from Agriculture to Manufacturing to Services or that choose not to improve value chain assets are leaving wealth on the table. Those countries satisfied with simple, balanced transactions are falling behind; they are walking away from opportunities to improve economies and the lives of those who live there.

Applying Opportunity-Based Economic Development (OBED) principles is a key part of the solution for countries seeking growth. Find what you're good at within each sector and focus on that, improving operations and technology for more superior transactions, wealth, and better lives. Move carefully and intentionally, and watch your economy grow.

The next chapter highlights the third OBED principle: that the move toward the Service sector will produce income inequality that must be addressed.

6

INCOME INEQUALITY: DEFINITION, CONSEQUENCES, CAUSES, AND SOLUTIONS

Income inequality is often one consequence of the move from Agriculture to Manufacturing to Services. Countries making this move can find themselves unbalanced, tipping toward heavy reliance on the asset of cheap labor that, as an economy grows, becomes less of an asset and more of a liability in the Manufacturing sector. We will look at what we found in our OBED study, explain what income inequality is and does, and offer remedies to the problem for developing countries eager to move forward.

Again, here is *Principle 3:* Once countries move toward more jobs in the Manufacturing sector, income inequality is generated. When countries move from Agriculture to Manufacturing to Services, the underlying asset of cheap labor in one sector doesn't yield a higher income level in the other with those same workers.

As a quick reminder from the study, the asset assigned to the Manufacturing sector was unschooled, cheap labor. But that cheap labor turned out to be both an asset and a liability. While there was a direct positive effect on Manufacturing sector growth, there was a negative effect on sector growth in purchasing power and income generation, two of the main macroeconomic indicators of a society at large. More products were being made, but workers' pay and/or standards of living did not improve. Those cheap laborers might have brought overall growth to the Manufacturing sector, but they didn't earn more money per capita in their jobs and thus contribute more to the economy.

We ran an extra regression to investigate this relationship, this time using the interaction between Manufacturing growth and the amount of highly skilled labor instead of unskilled labor. We used the asset from the Services sector, the mean years of education per capita, as the variable. The result was positive and significant, which indicates that having higher-educated people increases the per capita income earned in the Manufacturing sector for everyone.

It should come as no surprise that there is a large salary discrepancy between low-skilled and high-skilled workers in the Manufacturing sector. This rift, found in every country to varying degrees, is what we call *income inequality.*

Income is defined as a household's disposable means: employee earnings, self-employment income, capital income, remittances, with taxes and social security contributions deducted. That disposable income is divided by the number of people living in the household.[150] A household with two parents and five children earns less overall than a household with one parent, one child, and one grandparent because the disposable income is divided among seven people instead of three. There are also cases in which a larger family ends up wealthier than a smaller family living on the same income and in the same geographic location. If this is the case, it's often because the larger family manages its resources better to allow for more savings and investments. Each family's use of disposable income helps determine its level of wealth.

The *Gini coefficient*, developed by Italian statistician Corrado Gini in 1912, is used to gauge economic inequality by measuring income distribution in a population. The coefficient ranges from 0 to 1, with 0 representing perfect income equality and 1 representing perfect inequality. A country that has everyone earning the same income, which never happens, would have a Gini coefficient of 0. On the other hand, there are no countries with a straight 1 because no country has one person earning everything and everyone else earning nothing.[151]

The goal is for a country to be as close to 0 as possible in its Gini coefficient. The 36 OECD (Organization of Economic Cooperation and Development) member countries are ranked according to income inequality and poverty rate, which is tied to income inequality as many of the lowest-paid workers live below the poverty line. Costa Rica, with a Gini coefficient (GC) of 0.480, Mexico (0.459), South Africa (0.620), and Turkey (0.404) were among the highest. Among the lowest were Iceland (0.246), Finland (0.259), Belgium (0.268), and the Czech Republic (0.258). The United States had a GC of 0.391, Netherlands of 0.285, and South Korea of 0.295.[152]

Poverty Rate (PR) is defined as the ratio of the number of people whose income falls below the poverty line, which is half the median income of the total population. South Africa, with the highest GC, also has the highest poverty rate at 0.266. Iceland, with a low GC, has a total poverty rate of 0.065. The United States has a PR of 0.178.[153]

The Seven Pillars Institute, a nonprofit financial ethics organization, cites several disadvantages to countries with high economic (used interchangeably with *income*) inequality. Inequality stifles economic growth, increases crime, decreases health, increases political inequality, and lowers education levels. While the SPI also lists some advantages—drives growth, increases fairness—"the disadvantages of economic inequality are more numerous and arguably more significant than the benefits."[154]

"Some economists conclude inequality is beneficial overall for stimulating growth, improves the quality of life for all members of a society, or is merely a necessary part of social progress. Other economists claim wealth concentrations create perpetually oppressed minorities, exploit disadvantaged populations, hinder economic growth, and lead to numerous social problems," according to the article.[155]

SOUTH AFRICA'S HIGH INCOME INEQUALITY

A recent report from the World Bank calls South Africa "one of the most unequal countries in the world. Inequality is high, persistent and has increased since 1994" (the end of apartheid). Despite some gains in poverty reduction between 1994 and 2010, those gains were reversed between 2011 and 2015.[156] According to the report, "High levels of income polarization are manifested in very high levels of chronic poverty, a few high-income earners and a relatively small middle class. . . . Accelerating poverty and inequality reduction will require a combination of policies that seek to unlock the full potential of labor markets and promote inclusive growth through skilled job creation."[157]

Phiwe Budaza lives in Cape Town and struggles to make ends meet. She works as a bartender, for a company that rents cameras and film equipment, and as a freelance photographer. "It's hard for someone like me who doesn't have a full-time job to survive in Cape Town. The rent for an apartment [in the city] is like three times what I earn in a month," she said in a recent NPR story.[158]

The NPR story cites World Bank statistics that the top 1 percent of South Africans own 70.9 percent of the nation's wealth, with the bottom 60 percent collectively controlling 7 percent of the nation's wealth. The official unemployment rate is 27 percent. In 2015, 55.5 percent of South Africans survived on less than $5 a day.[159]

Looking more closely at the Manufacturing sector, South Africa's top 10 manufacturing categories, as of 2018, were meat, fish, fruits, etc.; coke, petroleum products, nuclear fuel; motor vehicles; iron and steel products; beverages; other chemical products; other food products; non-ferrous metal products; basic chemicals; and parts and accessories.[160] In fact, the sector grew 4.3 percent in 2017 thanks to increased production of products in food and beverages, petroleum, and iron and steel.[161]

While overall growth in South Africa is forecast, "extreme inequality has become a major constraint to higher levels of economic growth, because it is undermining policy certainty and depressing investment." The World Bank expects South Africa to keep to low-growth levels—1.4 percent in 2018, 1.8 percent in 2019, and 1.9 percent in 2019—because "slow growth and high inequality reinforce each other."[162]

South Africa is also hurt by its reliance on "casual" workers, or workers who work less than full time and so are afforded no medical benefits and no vacation. These workers earn sometimes half of what permanent workers earn.[163] In the second quarter of 2018, unemployment was at 26.7 percent; the Manufacturing sector gained 58,000 jobs and Agriculture lost 3,000. Youth unemployment was especially high.[164]

One source says that the average annual wage for low-skilled workers was 3,950 ZAR ($278 US), while the average wage for highly skilled workers was at 21,300 ZAR ($1,498 US).[165] Combine these low wages with stats that show 29 percent of the population in severe poverty, with four-fifth of the rural population living below the poverty line,[166] and it's clear what's behind South Africa's high GC.

"South Africa is really facing the triple challenge of poverty, unemployment, and inequality," said Nkosazana Dlamini-Zuma, former head of the African Union who now is part of President Cyril Ramaphosa's cabinet. "We are a relatively rich country but with a lot of poor people."[167]

The extreme income inequality in South Africa shows up in statistics presented at the Institute for African Alternatives Confronting Inequality conference. A National Income Dynamics Study showed that 29 percent of South Africans are in severe poverty, unable to "afford to buy food or access healthcare, decent sanitation, and other essentials of a dignified life."[168]

South Africa is an extreme example of the effects of income equality, with much of its population struggling to get by day to day. Even as a member of BRICS, a group of emerging economies including Brazil, Russia, India, China, and South Africa, the country has a long way to go. Yet income inequality affects all countries in one way or another.

INCOME INEQUALITY AROUND THE WORLD

The World Inequality Report 2018, drawn from data on the World Wealth and Income Database (WID.World), reports that income inequality "has increased rapidly in North America and Asia, has grown moderately in Europe, and has stabilized at extremely high levels in the Middle East, sub-Saharan Africa, and Brazil."[169]

In the United States, for example, the bottom 90 percent—nearly 145 million families—collectively own as much wealth as the roughly 161,000 families in the top 0.1 percent.[170] The top 10 percent of the population owns 77.2 percent of the wealth, with the bottom 90 percent owning 22.8 percent.[171] Income inequality in the U.S. is near the top among "rich" countries.[172]

Between 1980 and 2014, the pre-tax incomes of the bottom 50 percent of the population increased by only $200, from $16,400 to $16,600, though their post-tax incomes rose 21 percent during that time. Growth of the middle 40 percent saw a 42 percent pre-tax increase between 1980 and 2014, with a post-tax rise of 49 percent. Yet the average income for the top 10 percent doubled, and for the top 1 percent it tripled.[173]

Income Inequality

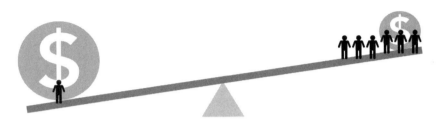

Income inequality isn't just statistics. It's real-life people trying to manage real-life problems that can seem insurmountable. The OECD created a report titled "How does income inequality affect our lives?" which offered several ways IE hurts economies and people. One of the main ways is that low-income families invest less in education and skills, which likely reduces the number of skilled workers able to work at higher-skilled jobs.[174] Wealthier families can afford to invest more in education, especially higher education, and there is a better chance for quality education at the elementary and high school levels as well, as schools with larger numbers of disadvantaged students don't attract as many high-qualified teachers and have a variety of other struggles.[175]

Other studies indicate that increased income inequality affects health in a variety of ways. Physical health is affected in terms of higher risk for early death, higher rates of obesity particularly in children, poorer mental health (depression, schizophrenia, other mental illnesses), and higher infant mortality.[176]

In the United States, healthcare costs are one aspect of income inequality. A recent piece in *The Atlantic* said that research "indicates that household spending on health care is a significant contributor to income inequality in the United States. It also indicates that medical expenses push millions of Americans below the federal poverty line."[177]

"Poor people," researchers found, "spent much more of their income on health care than the richest people did" and "medical spending sent millions of people effectively into poverty or into deeper rungs of poverty.... Even with Medicaid as a safety net, health care is a major burden for low-income people—so much so that it deeply exacerbates differences in income and wealth."[178]

Let's dig deeper into the mountain of problems created or exacerbated by income inequality. In under-developed countries, the problems are huge. In developed countries, the problems are just as huge but perhaps better hidden.

Basic needs for food, shelter, clean water, clothing, and education suffer when income inequality is out of control. In Haiti, my homeland, roughly a quarter of the people have no electricity and approximately 50 percent of the population uses unsanitary water. Only half of Haitian children attend school, and roughly 30 percent of the population is food insecure. Yet the top 20 percent of households hold 64 percent of the nation's wealth.[179]

When President Jovenel Moise announced in mid 2018 that fuel prices would increase, the population that lived on the financial edge protested. Riots ensued, perpetrated by people who could barely afford to feed their families and couldn't pay more for fuel to get them to their jobs, cook, and more. The fuel increase was revoked, but the response to it signified how close to the edge those in poverty live.

Parents in Haiti, struggling to provide food for their children on the poverty-level wages dad makes working in a small textile factory fifteen miles from home by bus, must now pay more per bus ride because fuel prices have gone up and buses pass along the cost. Less money is available for food and other basic supplies. Perhaps now those children can't attend school because their parents can't buy books or even shoes. Yet a family in the highest income bracket in Haiti simply pays more for the fuel and moves on with life. Income inequality makes the responses to one cost increase very different.

The link between poverty and income inequality is strong. A study done by LSE Works and CASE (Centre for Analysis of Social Exclusion) and others found that "levels of inequality and poverty are highly correlated" in the study of 26 European countries.[180] Drivers of this inequality/poverty issue included economic, political, social, and cultural mechanisms such as distribution of abilities, self-interest of the rich and powerful, values, beliefs, and fear.[181]

As the report states, "Demand shift in favour of high-skilled workers and a weakening in the wage bargaining power of low-skilled workers increases the risk of unemployment, low pay, and precarious employment for lower-skilled workers and increases wage inequality between skill levels."[182]

This statement supports our OBED finding that adding highly skilled workers increases GDP per capita but doesn't necessarily increase the quality of life of low-skilled workers. The results can be devastating for this group that brought growth to the Manufacturing sector but that isn't benefiting through higher pay and better overall lifestyle due to lack of bargaining power and an overabundance of cheap labor.

"The evidence suggests," according to the report, "that tackling poverty without addressing inequality will be ineffective in the long run unless the mechanisms that link the two are broken."[183]

What does that income inequality/poverty look like?

It looks like a poor, rural Chinese family struggling to feed itself on wages from a low-paying job or government assistance. It's a poor Haitian family selling mangoes from the backyard tree to pay for school uniforms. It's a near-retirement age man in Pittsburgh struggling with diabetes, having a hard time getting his medicine because the clinic is a forty-minute bus ride away. It's a young mom who feeds her children ramen noodles because it's the only food she can afford. Often these same people are working long hours in factories making low wages.

Poverty looks like limited access to health, dental, prenatal, and mental health care. It looks like lack of fresh fruits and vegetables in urban areas because grocery stores are located miles away in the suburbs. It looks like the huge slums that exist in big cities such as Cape Town, Nairobi, Mumbai, Karachi, and Mexico City. It's drinking unsafe water and facing diseases such as dysentery, cholera, and typhoid. It's segregation—based on race, social caste, tribe, religious sect—with minorities the majority of those who struggle. School buildings leak when it rains, have limited technology infrastructure, lack textbooks, and don't have enough qualified teachers. Income equality looks like civil unrest (remember Haiti and the fuel price increase?) as those in poverty struggle to make their voices heard.

OBED principles cannot be maximized when income inequality is high. There are few opportunities to move beyond basic transactions to superior ones for individuals and businesses; when balanced transactions founder and superior transactions don't exist, a country's economy can't grow. And when an economy can't grow, the people are stuck too.

Our conclusion is that in an economy with lots of cheap, low-skilled labor, this asset didn't improve people's lives. They worked cheap, but didn't live well. The main problem created by cheap labor in the Manufacturing sector is that the asset doesn't generate enough superior transactions. Workers don't learn skills that guarantee them better jobs at the best pay, and employers don't get the best level of work those employees are capable of. It's a lose/lose relationship that results in loss for the employees, the sector, and the economy in general. Many superior transactions are left on the table.

Cheap labor is, in fact, oxymoronic. Cheap labor yields no significant returns for employers, the Manufacturing sector, or the economy not because the workers are low-skilled, but because supply is bigger than demand for that labor. The price of labor, as in any other market, is dictated by supply and demand. Jobs requiring little or no skill mean anyone and everyone can have access to those jobs, generating surplus in the market. Cheap laborers are producing an abundance of low-margin, low-value products and reaping a low-income payment in terms of low salaries and few benefits for workers and low return for employers.

Workers who enter the Manufacturing sector face widening income inequality personally because those jobs don't provide a good enough income to live better and improved lives through things like better housing, better health care, and better education for their children. In fact, when a worker is vulnerable or disadvantaged that worker will remain so in the Manufacturing sector unless he or she learns a marketable skill that allows him or her to move up from those low-income jobs.

All that cheap labor, as we discovered, didn't directly affect the Manufacturing sector or the economy in general, but a highly skilled and educated labor pool did. That asset brought growth to the Manufacturing and Services sectors, and helped improve the overall GDP per capita for all workers.

As the world has moved down the path from Agriculture to Manufacturing to Services, income inequality produces very different qualities of life between sectors of people even though the world is wealthier today than ever before. Income inequality generates a host of lost opportunities for those on the wrong side of that inequality, including the inability to invest extra money for long-term gain and stability; the inability to save money for short-term expenses such as repairs, health emergencies, or better housing; and the inability to invest in education for their children and/or themselves.

When low-income workers can't invest in long-term savings plans, financial institutions lose potential interest and fees. When workers can't save money, no big purchases such as appliances and cars fuel the local economy. When education is out of the question, those workers and their children can't develop skills that help themselves and the economy.

While countries such as the United States, China, and Germany are well aware of the inequality and have taken steps to even it out, developing countries have to be aware as well and take appropriate measures to find a healthy balance of workers at all skill levels. These countries will benefit when they reach a healthy income level for all workers, avoiding the extremes of very low-paid workers and very highly paid workers.

China is a world leader in manufacturing and has experienced huge economic growth, and with that growth came marked income inequality. Researchers found that incomes are divided into two groups: those in the eastern and coastal provinces and Inner Mongolia, and the inner provinces, where people earned only 60 percent of those in the coastal provinces. The coastal dwellers also reap the rewards of owning capital, having more education, and population growth, which all play a role in widening the income inequality between the areas.[184] While extreme poverty in China is said to have been eradicated, there are many who are still very poor and have trouble accessing government help.[185]

While China's richest grow richer thanks to better access to financial accelerators and the ability to own businesses, the middle class is squeezed thanks to slow-growing wages overall. The poor struggle mightily, another offshoot of high income inequality.[186] Experts say that "ensuring social safety nets at the bottom rungs of society becomes ever more important to ensuring social stability."[187] China still has work to do in this area.

SOLUTIONS TO REDUCING INCOME INEQUALITY

The World Inequality Lab predicts that "if within-country inequality continues to rise as it has since 1980, then global income inequality

Solutions to Income Inequality

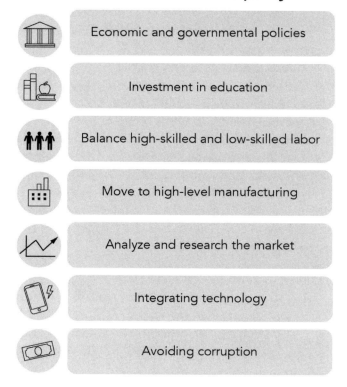

Economic and governmental policies

Investment in education

Balance high-skilled and low-skilled labor

Move to high-level manufacturing

Analyze and research the market

Integrating technology

Avoiding corruption

will rise steeply, even under fairly optimistic assumptions regarding growth in emerging countries. The global top 1 percent income share could increase from nearly 20 percent today to more than 24 percent in 2050, while the global bottom 50 percent share would fall from 10 percent to less than 9 percent."[188]

The WIL also projects that if all countries were to follow the United States' high-income inequality trajectory on track since 1980, the top 1 percent income share would reach 28 percent by 2050, with the bottom 50 percent share dropping to 6 percent. On the other hand, if countries were to follow the low-income inequality trajectory set in Europe, the top 1 percent share would decrease to 19 percent and the bottom 50 percent share would increase to 13 percent.[189]

These numbers indicate that countries individually and as part of the global economy must find ways to decrease income inequality. I'm sorry to say that there is no quick and easy solution to income inequality. I believe the best way to help solve the income inequality problem is for countries to anticipate and be proactive now. Many countries with current low income inequality had established policies and practices years ago to prevent it, whereas other countries did little or nothing years ago and now face the friction and troubles income inequality brings and must make corrections in real time.

I suggest the best way to tackle income inequality is to adopt a proactive approach even in the midst of an income inequality crisis. Within the Manufacturing sector, begin to establish a balanced climate in which the demand for labor does not outweigh the supply. When demand is greater than supply, low-skilled workers must settle for whatever wage they are offered, thereby eliminating the possibility of superior transactions that increased wages can bring.

There are several other ways to tackle this problem that threatens so many.

ECONOMIC AND GOVERNMENTAL POLICIES

Economic and governmental policies can help prevent income inequality. Among those are *income tax progressivity*, in which earners are taxed based on their ability to pay. Low-income earners have a lower tax rate than high-income earners, who pay more in taxes because they earn more. Called a progressive tax, this system reduces the tax burden on those who can least afford to pay, which leaves them more income to save, invest, and spend on education to improve their job futures.

"Evidence from recent inequality trends (for example, Brazil between 2000 and 2015) suggests that progressive tax reform should be given a higher priority in the future," according to the WID-World study.[190]

Another policy option is creation of a *global financial register* that keeps track of who and what entities own the world's wealth. Such a register would make it harder for entities to hide wealth in tax havens and financial securities such as equities and bonds, which allows them to evade taxation.

In 2013, Apple was in hot water after a U.S. Senate subcommittee inquiry concluded that the California-based company "had avoided tens of billions of dollars in taxes by shifting profits to Irish subsidiaries that the panel's chairman called 'ghost companies.'"[191]

Apple's CEO, Tim Cook, denied the actions, but when Ireland began to tighten its tax structure Apple moved its assets to Jersey, a small channel island that "typically does not tax corporate income."[192]

The *New York Times* story says, "Apple has accumulated more than $128 billion in profits offshore, and probably much more, that is untaxed by the United States and hardly touched by any other country."[193]

Apple isn't the only company to benefit, and the U.S. not the only country to lose out on collecting taxes that could benefit economies. The Organization for Economic Cooperation and Development estimates that "tax strategies like the ones used by Apple—as well as Amazon, Google, Starbucks, and others—cost governments around the world as much as $240 billion a year in lost revenue."[194]

While a global financial register "would deal a severe blow to financial opacity," entities "will not transfer information to authorities in the absence of regulations compelling them to do so."[195]

INVESTMENT IN EDUCATION

A second solution to income inequality and reducing a country's GC is investment in education. Countries, regions, cities, and even neighborhoods can see income inequality numbers reduced when more people, particularly young people, have access to quality education at all levels from pre-kindergarten through trade school and college. Education generally leads to better paying jobs, which leads to reduced income inequality.

One study indicates that the growing achievement gap between children in the United States has less to do with higher- versus lesser-educated parents, than it does with income differences between them. While the number of low-income high school graduates who enter college immediately has grown, half of them don't complete a degree within six years. The number is three-fifths for Hispanic and African American students.[196]

Governments can offer grants or low-interest loans to allow people to gain the skills they need to become highly skilled workers. The range of such workers is broad, from mechanics and plumbers to computer coders and paramedics. These kinds of jobs require additional training and can easily raise the income levels of workers.

Grants and loans help some, but school debt could have some students dropping out of college early. Student loan debt is at an all-time high in the U.S. at $1.5 trillion, with four in 10, roughly 42 percent, having taken out loans to pay for school. About 20 percent are behind on payments.[197]

Another part of the education equation is to make high school mandatory. Many developing countries don't require a high school diploma; doing so will allow entree into additional education and additional job skills.

Higher education—education above a high school level—often looks different than the usual four-year degree at a university. In the Netherlands, third-level education is offered at both vocational and academic levels. Vocational training, at a university of applied science or HBO, educates students for jobs in industry, health care, trade, social services, and the public sector. Academic education, at a university, educates students in the academic disciplines.[198]

A Dutch student can go directly from vocational training to a job, providing that student with the ability to repay any loans, find adequate housing, and begin contributing to the national economy, thanks to government grants, tuition, and revenue from contracts with third parties.[199]

High schools in the United States offer dual enrollment/concurrent enrollment programs, in which high school students can enroll in college classes with the goal of finishing college early. Other programs have high school students attending five years of high school, but graduating with a two-year associate's degree from a local community college. Colleges and universities are helping students acquire real-world experience in their fields of study through internship programs and work-study programs.

Access to education is a key way to tighten the income inequality gap. As workers get needed education—through on-the-job training, vocational schools, community colleges, and universities—they acquire better jobs and earn more, thus contributing to the economy.

BALANCE HIGH-SKILLED AND LOW-SKILLED LABOR

A third way to lower a country's Gini coefficient is to find the balance between high-skilled and low-skilled labor and jobs. Every country needs a healthy balance between low-skilled and high-skilled workers. No country can grow economically and produce superior transactions if the majority of its workforce is contributing nothing to the economy because wages are subsistence level or lower.

My home country, Haiti, has 38 percent of its labor force working in Agriculture, 11.5 percent in Industry, about 50 percent in Services (these jobs include many small-scale vendors, cleaning and maintenance people, and so on),[200] with unemployment and underemployment rampant. One estimate says that more than two-thirds of the labor force doesn't have a formal job.[201] Compare these numbers to Germany, which has 1.4 percent of its labor force working in Agriculture, 24.4 percent in Industry, and almost 75 percent in Services. Unemployment is at 3.8 percent. It's easy to see which country has the most people contributing the most to the overall economy, and it's clear which economy is better overall: Germany, of course, which is the fifth largest in the world in terms of PPP, and is Europe's largest.[202]

Countries eager to reduce their Gini coefficients must find the balance between low-skilled, lower-paying jobs and higher-skilled, higher-paying jobs. That balance can be sought through loosening policies to allow high-skill businesses to operate easily in the country, looking for foreign direct investment, using accelerators to encourage growth in businesses already there, and increasing educational opportunities, all things we've already discussed.

MOVE TO HIGH-LEVEL MANUFACTURING

A fourth way to lower income inequality is to move away from low-level manufacturing to high-level manufacturing; to move from low-margin manufacturing such as textiles to high-margin manufacturing such as computer components. Higher margins allow for higher salaries, which makes for increased GDP per capita.

Also along these lines is to move from creating consumer goods to creating capital goods. There is a much higher margin when building machine parts sold to car makers than in making T-shirts sold to Target or H&M.

South Korea made this change starting in the 1970s, moving from industries such as textiles, clothing, and plywood to heavy industries (with higher profit margins) such as iron and steel, petrochemicals, and refined oil. The government helped move along this change with huge capital investment in these areas.[203] South

Korea currently has a GDP per capita of $37,740 and an unemployment rate of 3.7 percent.[204]

The move to high-level manufacturing is likely accompanied by governmental policies that attract these types of industries, access to financial accelerators and foreign direct investment, and training programs that allow workers to learn skills needed for these jobs.

ANALYZE AND RESEARCH THE MARKET

A fifth way to help lower income equality is to analyze and research the market to attract high-level investment and jobs. At a city, state, and country level, look hard at cutting-edge industries and find ways to attract them to your area. This can be through tax incentives, financial accelerators such as low-interest loans, and easily available land on which to build facilities.

It can also mean incentivizing the assets you already have, such as educational institutions to train workers; a good transportation system including access to expressways, airports, water ports, and rail lines; large tracts of land; technology infrastructure; and large numbers of workers.

Amazon made headlines in its search for a new headquarters. More than 238 cities in North America sent proposals to the e-commerce giant, offering tax incentives and other value-added incentives.[205] I will guarantee that those 238 cities maximized their assets and created as many incentives as possible in their proposals. As of this writing, the field had been narrowed to 20 metro areas—from Los Angeles to Miami, from Toronto, Canada, to Denver—as Amazon promises it will spend $5 billion there and employ 50,000.[206]

INTEGRATING TECHNOLOGY

Another way to avoid or help fix income inequality is technology integration. This can occur in all sectors, such as that done in the Agriculture sector (more food produced as use of technology rises) and the Manufacturing sector (computers and robotics doing more of the work once done by hand, thus increasing productivity), and at all levels. Industries will not come to a country in which internet access is intermittent, cell phone services cover only small areas, the electrical grid is archaic, and workers, skilled and unskilled, have no computer training nor opportunities to get it.

This integration begins at a grade-school level. Children must have access to basic technology in order to become familiar with it, learn from it, and, later, use it to aid their job search and marketable skills.

The Pew Research Center reported that nearly half of all households in the United States did not have access to high-speed internet at home, and nearly a third don't own a smartphone.[207] "With new computers and automation increasingly permeating not only manufacturing but all services, those with less familiarity with or access to the Internet, computers, and smartphones are left at a considerable disadvantage," according to *Business Insider*, which used the Pew Center research in a report.[208] It continues, "How should the United States address the issue of technological inequality? Early intervention is the key, experts say. That means giving kids from lower-income households ample access to connectivity and devices, even if it means direct subsidies to poorer and/or more remote areas."[209]

Says Zia Qureshi of The Brookings Institution, "technology policies must be reformed so that they promote innovation and wide diffusion" and "access to quality education and training must be greatly improved, including putting in place stronger and smarter programs for worker upskilling and reskilling and lifelong learning to respond to the shifting demand for skills."[210]

AVOIDING CORRUPTION

One final way to avoid income inequality is to avoid corruption. When those at the top steal from those at the bottom, income inequality is exacerbated. Inequality.org says, "Large-scale diversions of public funds are a particularly egregious mechanism through which corruption drives inequality. . . . Corrupt patronage networks can prevent fair access to economic and political power, serving to further the wealth and power of ruling elites, exacerbating inequality."[211]

Corruption on a large scale is just as heinous as corruption at a local level. The website cites mothers in Zimbabwe denied vaccinations for their children unless illegal "consultation fees" are paid, and families in Cameroon whose children could be expelled from school because they couldn't pay illegal fees demanded by the headmaster.[212]

Corruption can include rigging the bidding process on large projects, cutting corners on safety by paying bribes to inspectors, submitting fraudulent bills to Medicare, and even questionable lobbying activities.

CONCLUSION

The OBED study showed that the move from Agriculture to Manufacturing resulted in growth in the sector as industries employed more people and produced more goods. The asset in the Manufacturing sector—cheap, unskilled labor—fueled the growth in the sector. But the study also showed that sector growth didn't mean more per capita income growth for those unskilled workers.

The disparity between income earned by low-skilled and high-skilled workers generates income inequality, both a local and a global problem. Low-skilled workers toil long hours at factory jobs and barely get by on their salaries, while high-skilled workers make more money and work fewer hours. Who has more opportunity to make superior transactions? The workers who make more money, of course. What businesses have more opportunity to make superior transactions? Those that invest in higher-skilled workers in skilled jobs, making products with higher returns.

Developing countries will do well to be aware of the struggles and pitfalls of income inequality, some of which are listed in this chapter, and look for proactive ways to combat income inequality. Among the ways to do so are setting economic and governmental policies that foster higher-wage manufacturing jobs; investing in education at all levels; creating a balance between high- and low-skilled jobs; moving toward high-level manufacturing and toward capital instead of consumer goods; analyzing the market to attract high-level industries and workers; integrating technology into all levels of manufacturing; and putting an end to corruption.

Countries taking these steps will begin the journey toward better economies and better lives for the country's workers.

7

PURSUING SEVA: SUPERIOR ECONOMIC VALUE ADDED

My homeland, Haiti, was hit by a devastating earthquake in 2010, which brought the country to its knees. Not long after the earthquake, I created Trinity Lodge with American investor Jack Van Der Ploeg, which offers space for groups of up to twenty-five people to use for retreats and such, as well as a section of rooms for individuals. Several years later, Trinity Lodge grew to accommodate fifty people. I also started a movement to connect Haitian businesses with the many NGOs operating in the country, especially post-earthquake, with the hope that NGOs would purchase goods from Haitian businesses. To date, seven editions of the Buy Haitian, Restore Haiti initiative, created through Partners Worldwide when I was a manager there, have been organized and millions of dollars' worth of contracts obtained between Haitian businesses and NGOs.

Unfortunately, these successes were insufficient. Most Haitian businesses didn't have enough capital to retool, supply, and market their products to tap into the NGO market. Bridge Capital, owned by myself and two other investors, Fred Eppright and Reagan Stricklin, started providing Haitian businesses with the capital to reach into those markets, but in the last two years the NGOs began to slow down their work in Haiti.

We started revamping Bridge Capital for different opportunities. We could have continued to invest in those companies and kept making loans, but we decided to try a different tack by offering dollars for shares of companies. Recently we held a forum that brought seven Haitian businesses together to pitch their ideas to foreign investors. The first-ever Foreign Direct Investment Forum held in Haiti in September 2018 resulted in more than $2.2 million in FDI pledged toward four of the seven companies that pitched their ideas.

Each of those four companies that receive FDI from United States investors will accelerate their wealth creation, hopefully add employees and increase production, and eventually add to the economy of Haiti as a whole. Each business already added significant value thanks to media coverage, connections made with other businesses and U.S. investors, and knowledge gained on how to present the business to others. The goal is for the value added via FDI to grow and expand not only the business but the Haitian economy as a whole.

Accelerators such as FDI, which we talked about in an earlier chapter, take basic transactions and make them bigger and better. The initial investment, however, needs to be transformed through work to repay the investment and hopefully create more wealth to be shared with the wider economy. That wealth is shared thanks to additional taxes paid by the business and workers, workers injecting increased pay into the banking system as they save more and into the local economy as they spend more, and other investment into society such as donations to nonprofits, more time to volunteer, and increased leadership roles in local decision-making bodies.

In fact, the FDI received by these companies is just the first step in a long process of adding value to the company and the economy. The added value is called *economic value added* (EVA) and is the path of wealth creation that happens in the context of individual businesses and larger economies. The idea is reflected in our fourth principle.

Principle 4: Transactions are key to business growth. Focusing on meaningful, market-based transactions brings superior returns as businesses generate wealth, which creates more opportunities and more resources that create value for the business and society as a whole, without causing income inequality or other societal problems.

Balanced transactions occur when both the buyer and the seller are satisfied. A bakery sells a loaf of bread for $2, making $1 in profit. The buyer is satisfied with the bread and is fine with paying $2 for it. The bakery can also make wheat bread, if there is demand, at a cost of $1.10 per loaf for the bakery that uses the same number of employees and the same oven to make the bread. It then charges $2.50 for a loaf of wheat bread. The bakery makes $1.40 profit per loaf. When the bakery added wheat bread to meet customer demand, it increased profit margin by .40 cents per loaf overall for all breads.

Another example of economic value added comes when the bakery begins offering one free chocolate chip cookie with each bread purchase, delighting the mother who gives the cookie to her youngster, then buys a dozen chocolate chip cookies when she returns to the bakery two days later. That one sample cookie increased revenue for the bakery.

EVA also happens when the same bakery begins to sell coffee along with the bread, tempting customers with the aroma of ground beans and a quick cup of coffee to revive their energy. Soon customers are stopping by just for coffee, buying bread as long as they are there. The bakery, knowing they have a great customer base, increases the price of a loaf of white bread to $2.25 and wheat bread to $2.75 and nobody complains because they're also getting great coffee and maybe even cookies. The overall experience of visiting that bakery has turned from the simple task of buying bread to the pleasant experience of a good cup of coffee, a chocolate chip cookie, and good bread to take home.

The bakery is selling more bread at the higher price, while lowering the cost of making that bread by baking in bigger batches, which costs less per unit made. Revenue rises with the economy of scale. In the language of OBED, the bakery has moved from basic transactions to superior transactions, thereby not only creating economic value added but creating *superior* economic value added (SEVA). These are examples of a business creating SEVA from a positive return on investment.

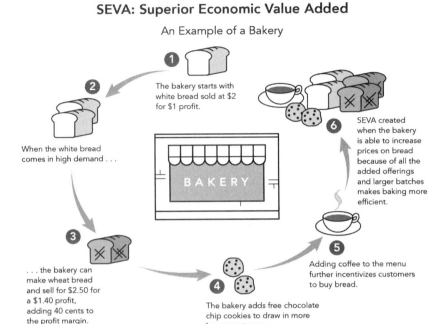

SEVA: Superior Economic Value Added

An Example of a Bakery

① The bakery starts with white bread sold at $2 for $1 profit.

② When the white bread comes in high demand . . .

③ . . . the bakery can make wheat bread and sell for $2.50 for a $1.40 profit, adding 40 cents to the profit margin.

④ The bakery adds free chocolate chip cookies to draw in more happy customers.

⑤ Adding coffee to the menu further incentivizes customers to buy bread.

⑥ SEVA created when the bakery is able to increase prices on bread because of all the added offerings and larger batches makes baking more efficient.

The question we ask ourselves is how the use of accelerators allows businesses to create superior value added while also benefiting society as a whole. Does the extra growth and profit at the business level accelerate society's economic growth even more? I say the answer is yes.

As I say in my first book *From Aid to Trade*, "Business owners apply OBED when they pursue opportunities to provide goods and services that satisfy customer needs profitably. However, the application of OBED is as relevant for individual enterprises as it is for entire sectors and the market as a whole. As in Adam Smith's theory of the invisible hand, when combined, every single marketable opportunity pursued shapes the market as a whole. Therefore, OBED promotes the use of balanced transactions as the best way to fulfill needs in the society."[213]

We've talked about how countries can move from an Agriculture- to a Manufacturing-based society and what the move can look like, as well as at least one of the pitfalls—economic inequality—of that move. Now I'd like to move from the negative to the positive by helping businesses and economies learn the principles of *economic value added*. I want to share how the move from economic value added

(EVA) to superior economic value added (SEVA) creates superior wealth not only for businesses, but also for society as a whole.

Economic Value Added (EVA) is a measure of financial performance based on profit after what is paid out in capital; it is calculated by deducting the cost of running the business from its total revenue. Basically, it's the return on the investment. For our purposes, SEVA is the OBED principle of moving from balanced to superior transactions with the goal of further creating more opportunities for the businesses, the country, and its people.

FROM BUSINESS TO SOCIETY

Adam Smith (1723–1790) was a Scottish economist who changed the face of economics forever. He is best known for his *An Inquiry into the Nature and Causes of the Wealth of Nations* (1776), which turned on its head the old view of a nation's wealth being only its stock of gold and silver. Then, countries taxed imports, subsidized exports, and protected domestic industries. These policies applied to countries and cities, which did their best to prevent anything from destabilizing their own producers of goods.[214]

Smith turned all that around, arguing that free exchange benefited both the buyer and seller. Trade, he posited, benefits both sides as it increases prosperity. A nation's wealth lies in its total production and commerce, what we call today gross national product (GNP).[215] Smith's treatise provided the foundation for the nineteenth-century era of free trade and economic expansion. He knew that prosperity grew best in an open and competitive marketplace.[216]

The free trade that benefits individuals, businesses, and countries at large is the basis of OBED's structures and the findings in the study. Each sector we studied had an underlying asset that could be leveraged into superior transactions; when superior transactions were achieved—using a variety of accelerators —countries and individuals benefited.

Adam Smith also argued that businesses will be more efficient, and thus gain wealth, when production tasks are broken down into smaller tasks done by people who have been trained to do those tasks specifically.[217] Smith called this *specialization*, or division of labor. So, a tool-and-die company trains a percentage of its workers on a particular die-making machine, with those workers running that machine efficiently and well, thus saving time and money and increasing production. Other workers are trained on different machines, also saving time and increasing production. While workers may cross-train, each specializes on one machine. It's the idea of being really good at a few things instead of half good at a lot of things. In business, that "really good" means a better-running business.

Ann Byle, who contributed to this book, recently signed on as a consultant to a business that helps authors complete their books, contact publishers, build platforms, and reach their specific readers on social media. Ann isn't experienced in (and doesn't even like) doing all of those things, but is trained and experienced in some of them. Instead of slogging through the world of social media, confused and exasperated, she will focus her consultant energies on writing press releases, crafting book proposals, and copy-editing manuscripts.

The business gains from her expertise because it can market her skills, clients gain by having an expert work on their project, and Ann gains when she's paid. The business practices good EVA principles by adding specific expertise in the form of consultants to its roster and advertising its services to potential clients. It achieves SEVA by breaking down tasks and assigning them to the most skilled consultants, thus accelerating how much work the business can take on and turning the work around quickly.

Everyone gains: the business collects fees and gains credibility; Ann uses her expertise to make money; clients get the products they need to further their careers; publishers look at a quality book project and perhaps agree to publish it; and the end users, readers, get just the book they want.

The official term for this is *work specialization*, or sometimes *division of labor*. One of the goals of such specialization is increased productivity. As workers get better and better at one task, they are able to move faster and accomplish more, thus increasing production. The owner of a painting business may find that one employee is especially good at detailed trim work, while another excels at doing ceilings and/or walls. The paint job gets done faster and with fewer mistakes when the trim guy does the trim work and the wall guy does only the walls. Not that each couldn't do the other's job; it's using the best people for the job that fits them best.

Superior economic value added (SEVA) occurs when an already-profitable company can cut down on time and effort spent on tasks it already accomplishes, further accelerating productivity. SEVA means going from basic productivity to superior productivity by leaving no untapped opportunity on the table that can add economic value. SEVA seeks optimization of market equilibrium between supply and demand.

Another of Smith's themes is that the future depends on capital accumulation now that is protected and managed well.[218] This idea relates back to the need for government policies that protect and encourage capital creation, as well as putting an end to corruption that siphons off capital into the hands of corrupt individuals or entities. We could write a whole book on this topic, which we'll address in part in the next chapter. In the meantime, know that businesses must protect and manage their assets—cash and other monetary capital, human capital, buildings, machinery, and so on—to allow for growth in the future.

Adam Smith, an economist who lived 250 years ago, is still relevant today; the principles he wrote about are the bedrock of many of the OBED principles we've talked about. When businesses add superior economic value and begin to flourish, so does the overall economy. The economy is nourished by business, much like an unborn child is nourished by a mother who looks to her own health first and, thus, the health of her child.

To take the mother/child metaphor further, the mother can provide even more nourishment to her child by eating better and taking prenatal vitamins. She can eat average food and provide average nutrients to her baby, which is fine. But by consuming better than average food and vitamins, she can add superior value/health to her child. On the other hand, she can remove value by drinking alcohol, ignoring prenatal vitamins, smoking, doing drugs, and eating badly.

Businesses, too, can make the choice to stay average and exist on basic transactions. Businesses can also hurt themselves and society by making bad financial decisions, not using accelerators, or straying outside the law. Or businesses can take advantage of accelerators of all kinds to increase productivity and thus profit. These are the businesses that create superior economic value added, and make society wealthier because of it.

Two of the experts in the field of economic development are Michael Porter and David Ricardo. Porter—economist, teacher at Harvard Business School, expert on competitiveness—is well known for his "five basic forces" model of business strategy. The original article outlining the five basic forces ran in the March 1979 issue of the *Harvard Business Review*.[219] The five forces are:

· Threat of new entrants

· Bargaining power of customers

· Threat of substitute products or services

· Bargaining power of suppliers

· Jockeying for position among current competitors

"The collective strength of these forces determines the ultimate profit potential of an industry," he said in the HBR article.[220] "Knowledge of these underlying sources of competitive pressure provides the groundwork for a strategic agenda of action."[221]

An in-depth study of Porter's work is impossible here, but his principles, especially as related to competitive advantage, apply to our OBED strategy of discovering where a business is strongest and using that strength to create superior economic value added. As a business looks at the five factors outlined by Porter, it can see its strengths and weaknesses, discover where it can be competitive, and use that competitiveness to lead to SEVA.

Digicel is a mobile communications company that has found its niche in Central America, the Caribbean, and the Asia Pacific region by serving thirty-one markets. Digicel serves 4.8 million Haitian individuals and businesses, offering Haitians easy-access mobile phone and telecommunications plans thanks to more than $1 billion in FDI into the country. According to chairman Maarten Boute, investment in Haiti by Digicel represented 20 percent of the country's GDP growth in its first five years there.[222]

That growth came not just from the initial FDI, but also from post-earthquake FDI, a "double down on the country" into rural areas with $220 million additional investment.[223] Digicel employs around 1,000 direct employees and roughly 65,000 out on the streets selling airtime to phone users.[224]

Digicel created *superior economic value added* through its use of FDI, an accelerator, to help solve the communication problem in

Haiti while contributing to the Haitian economy on many levels. The 65,000 employees out in the streets usually have a main source of income and work for Digicel on the side, thus maximizing their income and then pouring it into the local economy. Digicel's direct employees also earn a livable wage, allowing them to contribute via taxes and purchasing power.

In general, Digicel has contributed to solving the communication problem in Haiti, as well as injecting $1 billion into one of the smallest economies in the world. The business innovated by introducing its prepaid phone system and also in how it distributes the minutes for those phones. Instead of using computers and the Internet as the only source for buying minutes, Digicel leveraged the younger population who were eager to make money, understood the technology, and were free to roam the streets and countryside selling those phone minutes. Many work for Digicel in this capacity, which provides income to them which they can inject into the economy.

Digicel, owned by Dennis O'Brien, has increased SEVA by positioning itself as a top telecommunications provider, and helped increased SEVA in businesses that can make more trades and transactions thanks to reliable telecommunications. Without that additional $1 billion in FDI, Haiti's economy would be $1 billion smaller.

Schools can use the cell phone service, available reliably thanks to Digicel, to increase educational opportunities, while individuals can use the technology to access mobile banking, search and apply for jobs, and communicate with friends and family. With the additional income the Digicel street vendors earn, they can afford better education, health care, and food.

A local company could decide to start a cell phone company to offer an alternative to Digicel, but it wouldn't be nearly as big and add nearly as much to the economy. When a large company such as Digicel decides to invest in a small country such as Haiti, the boost to the economy is huge and benefits all, thanks to SEVA.

David Ricardo, a contemporary of Adam Smith, developed the theory of "comparative advantage," the idea that "a country [that] trades for products it can get at a lower cost from another country is better off than if it had made the products at home."[225] His is subtle thinking. Comparative advantage occurs when the benefits of purchasing goods from a business (or country) outweigh the disadvantages. For instance, many businesses buy the services of call centers in India, weighing the disadvantage of workers not speaking English clearly with the advantage of much cheaper costs. Any company can use comparative advantage to its own advantage, thus creating SEVA. One recent report suggested that Haiti would have comparative advantage in BPO (Business Process Outsourcing) related to call centers, citing Haiti's low labor costs and large pool of young, multilingual workers.[226]

Let's say that a large book distribution company wants to open a call center to serve its many customers across the Caribbean, Central America, and the United States. After researching the cost of setting up a center in the United States, the company decides to look abroad, settling on Haiti after a presentation by Business Solutions Inc., a new firm started by young Haitian professionals whose dream is to boost the economic advantages of their homeland. They present the superior economic value added that their company promises: young employees who know technology, quick call turnaround, knowledge of the book industry, reduced labor costs, multilingual employees, and reduced rent and utilities costs.

The distribution company compares the cost of labor and other overhead between the U.S. and Haiti, as well as the potential disadvantages of locating in Haiti, including insecure electrical and telecommunications grids and potential corruption that could siphon funds. But the advantages outweigh the disadvantages and Business Solutions Inc. is awarded the contract. It used its superior economic value added to land a huge, lucrative contract. Assets—young workforce, multilingual workers, lower overhead—became advantage when utilized wisely. The distribution company sought out comparative advantage and chose the Haitian company.

Smith, Ricardo, and Porter each highlight theories that are the bedrock of OBED—comparative advantage, competitive advantage, specialization—and undergird OBED's principle of using assets to highest advantage to increase productivity and wealth. Our research shows that assets become advantage when those assets are used wisely to increase EVA; when every economic opportunity is seized regarding those assets, SEVA results. And when a business prospers, so does the overall economy—as Smith, Ricardo, and Porter knew.

Take vetiver, for example. Vetiver is a plant known for its quality medicinal oils and a source of income for small farmers in Haiti.[227] The perennial's oil is used to treat anxiety and brain health, and is widely used in making perfume, but the health of the vetiver industry is in trouble because of outdated farming techniques.[228] The plant is harvested by digging the whole thing out, which over the years has led to soil degradation and erosion.[229] Now farmers worry that, with the top soil gone, they may not be able to grow vetiver any longer.[230]

UniKode, one of Haiti's top vetiver oil producers, is working with farming cooperatives to help farmers grow and harvest better crops. Farmers such as Pierre Sonore in rural Tricon are learning to use natural erosion-control barriers to enhance his soil and thus his crop.[231] One of Haiti's largest exports is perfumes and cosmetics which use vetiver, at 15.5 percent of all exports, with the country exporting $26.9 million dollars' worth in 2016.[232] Haiti grows 50 percent of the 120–150 tons of vetiver oil produced worldwide.[233]

UniKode, whose website calls it "Home of 100% pure vetiver oil from Haiti,"[234] produces vetiver oil from the roots supplied by 16,000 farmers each year.[235] The company helped farmers group into co-ops and helped them learn and use sustainable farming practices to increase crop production, which had been waning.[236]

"UniKode recognizes that to build substantive change into the system, modifications and improvements must be researched, designed, managed, supervised, and documented. These added values and qualities should be supported at all levels of the value chain," it says.[237]

That paragraph alone points to numerous potential economic value-added steps, as well as superior economic value-added steps. UniKode, a producer of vetiver oil that is exported to companies that make essential oils, needs vetiver from farmers. Farmers are having trouble producing enough crop, so UniKode steps in to help educate and train farmers in new techniques. As a result, farm-ers raise more and better vetiver crops and UniKode creates more vetiver oil to export.

Instead of simply relying on the crops the farmers provided, UniKode took the next step to teach them better methods. UniKode provided SEVA by helping farmers learn new methods to increase production. The farmers also provided SEVA by applying those methods and increasing their crop production. As the farmers increased production and wealth, so UniKode increased production and wealth; and Haiti's economy improved regionally and nationwide.

Businesses that don't produce a crop like vetiver or other goods can create SEVA by offering training and seminars that could mean additional growth in sales. If a salesperson is selling 100 windows a month, providing decent EVA, but after a training seminar sells 150 windows a month with the same amount of time and effort, that salesperson has reached SEVA.

OBED LINK IS STRONG

In our research based on OBED principles, we have been able to establish the direct link between *superior economic value added* and benefits to society. When businesses turn assets into profit through transactions, society reaps some of those rewards.

In the Agriculture sector we found a "positive and highly significant" relationship between growth in the sector and growth in the economy in general, though that growth was related to transactions and not merely the amount of agricultural land in a country. Every time businesses turned that arable land into marketable opportunities, the sector added value to the overall economy.

The same positive relationship between a country's economic growth and sector growth was found in Manufacturing and Services sectors, particularly when measured against the presence of more highly skilled workers in the sectors. As businesses in these sectors grew and added economic value, they also added value to the economy as a whole.

The "invisible hand" theory posited by economist Adam Smith isn't just an old hypothesis to be discarded as outdated; it's as relevant today as it was when Smith conceived it generations ago. It has been proven in our research, which showed significant alignment effects and positive outcomes, and fits into OBED's view that assets in themselves don't help the economy. It's when they are being transformed into economic opportunity that they create value.

The market system that exists in most countries is based on transactions and supply-and-demand, through which economic value is added and positive returns on investments occur. When transactions are made that bring positive return, this constitutes new wealth for business owners, who can then continue to invest in new businesses or grow the current ones, thus contributing to society in incremental ways.

The same way, when businesses maximize the opportunities they have by moving beyond basic transactions to superior ones that create superior value—by using accelerators to optimize opportunities—they create superior economic value added. Business owners not only have more resources to invest in their businesses, they also have two, three, or four times more resources to create a bigger economic impact on society.

That economic impact, thanks to improved economic value, can look many different ways. Businesses are able to provide better support for employees through better health care and connections to social services such as counseling or child care; more tax dollars flowing into the government can help fund better roads; and more funding becomes available for environmental research, cultural activities, and educational opportunities in area schools. All these things contribute to the improved well-being of society in general.

Can one small business make a difference? A small coffee shop may not make a huge impact on society, but with SEVA that coffee shop can create a higher percentage impact for its size than a coffee shop that sticks to EVA levels. Think about one drop of rain. That one drop of rain does almost nothing; but when that one drop is combined with a million others, the rain helps provide water for crops, rivers, big cities, and small villages. Much is accomplished when small drops (or businesses) merge with other drops to create a bigger and better whole.

This occurs at local and national levels. That small coffee shop can create SEVA and begin to impact its neighborhood; a giant manufacturing firm can create SEVA and impact a city; one segment of the Manufacturing sector can impact a nation. Each plays a role proportionate to its size and impact.

Think about Detroit, Michigan, and its metro area in the heyday of the automobile industry. The city was a mecca of industrialization including the mighty automotive industry. The Ford Motor Company and its Ford Factory was the largest of 125 car factories in the city during the early twentieth century.[238] The population had grown from under 80,000 in 1870 to over 1.5 million in 1930.[239] Cars, cars, and more cars poured off the assembly lines in the years after World War II. Thousands upon thousands of jobs helped fuel the economy thanks to good incomes, a strong tax base, and other industries that thrived alongside the automotive juggernaut. Residents could afford better housing, better education, and better health care, and tax dollars poured into the government to help fund roads, police and fire protection, and civic enterprises such as museums and sports arenas. The superior economic value added created a vital city and citizenry, not to mention the myriad automotive suppliers around the state and the country that also thrived and created jobs and SEVA.

Compare the mid twentieth-century Detroit with the struggling Detroit today, especially after the 2008–2009 economic crisis. Many of the high-skilled automotive jobs are gone and many neighborhoods have become wastelands. Many residents face poverty, failing schools, and limited services. While it isn't in the scope of this book to analyze the whys and wherefores of the struggling automotive industry, I can say that when transactions between the automotive industry and its customers began to wane and production slowed or ceased, the whole economy of the region suffered.

When jobs disappeared, so did salaries. When salaries disappeared, so did the ability to support schools, grocery stores, clothing stores, dry cleaners, restaurants, hardware stores, and so on. When businesses closed, the government couldn't collect taxes so roads fell into disrepair, school funding dropped, and hospitals and clinics struggled. There was no EVA because there was no economy to speak of.

Detroit is seeing somewhat of a resurgence today as businesses and individuals begin to reinvest in the city and its neighborhoods. Several automotive manufacturers that were bailed out by the government are in operation. Hopefully those businesses will see a return on their investments, and thus create superior economic value added.

It is clear through our research, through looking at history, and through observation of everyday life that businesses add value to society. When those businesses make basic transactions, *economic value added* (profit) helps the business and society. When those businesses move to superior transactions, as OBED suggests, *superior economic value added* occurs and benefits all of society in even more significant ways.

The more SEVA that businesses create, the better off society is.

8

POVERTY CREATION: THE "INVISIBLE HAND" IN REVERSE

My home country of Haiti is considered one of the poorest in the world. Despite its many assets—affordable labor pool, miles of beaches, historical sites, proximity to the United States, excellent climate for agriculture—most of Haiti's citizens live in extreme poverty and its economy is struggling at best. My goal for this book and my first book, *From Aid to Trade*, is to help bring Haiti and other struggling countries out of poverty into wealth.

Poverty is the inability to maximize potential, whether in an individual or a country. All the assets in the world can be present, but if those assets aren't maximized then poverty can result. Let's say a woman is gifted in mathematics; if she is denied education in mathematics and fails to secure a job in the mathematics field, instead finding a job working in a low-end retail store or factory, she experiences poverty due to low pay. That poverty could have been prevented if she had been able to maximize her potential in mathematics.

Yet if the demand for workers in her current job is higher than supply, she could create some wealth and even superior wealth. That wealth could be harder to achieve, however, because she may have to work extra hard and receive additional training because the job isn't within her aptitude. It's always more efficient, more effective, and less risky when someone can leverage his or her natural talents to learn a skill and perform well in a job within a field of knowledge. That doesn't mean individuals cannot find jobs outside their natural skills; it's just harder.

A person's natural talents and learned skills may not be in high demand in the current market or those talents/skills don't create enough income to break even or exceed needs. The individual can decide to target high-paying customers or jobs within his skills and work hard toward that goal, learn a new skill in a high-demand area that is outside her natural talents, or create a combination of both that allows him or her to generate enough wealth to meet or exceed his or her needs. That person has transformed his or her assets.

This brings us to *Principle 5:* Simply having assets and (perceived) liabilities does not guarantee economic transformation. Those assets and liabilities must be transformed into meaningful transactions. Without that transformation, societies may become poor and troubled despite possessing valuable assets.

UNTRANSFORMED OPPORTUNITIES

Deficiency results when opportunities are not transformed or transformed in the wrong way. With our female mathematician, her needs—food, clothing, education, transportation, health care—are unmet due to the gap between the size of the needs and the size of the resources available to meet those needs because of her unmet potential.

If the total cost of living for one person is $10 a day—including transportation, food, lodging, education, and so on—but that person only generates $5 a day, in this book's terms that person is generating $5 worth of poverty every day. This negative return or *negative value added* forces this person into a $5 loss for society. Multiply that one person by millions; the more people who accumulate deficiencies, or losses, the poorer that society becomes.

On the other hand, when a person's income is enough to cover their expenses they achieve a break-even level, to borrow a business term. This means the person generates exactly enough revenue to cover his or her expenses. If total expenses are $10 and total revenue is $10, that person generates neither poverty nor wealth. Making $1 less means he or she generates $1 worth of poverty, and $1 more means generating $1 worth of wealth, or value added. The first step toward self-sustainability is generating more wealth than the cost of expenses.

Self-sustainability is achieved when a person owns or can purchase everything he or she needs for financial well-being. It is achieved when that person earns not only enough to allow them to break even, but enough to cover future expenses such as saving for retirement and purchasing a home. Self-sustainability also means earning enough to make mortgage payments, to pay for upkeep on a home and/or vehicle (including a replacement if necessary), vacations, gifts, leisure expenses, insurance, and retirement contributions.

Depending on the country, individuals face more or less challenge in achieving self-sustainability, yet the goal for each citizen is to reach that level if he or she wants to remain a viable and economically valuable member of society.

There isn't a way for a person to live and not have needs to be met. Being is spending. Needs don't leave, and poverty isn't going to wait. It behooves us to look hard at what needs are present and how those needs can be met in a way that avoids deficiencies and poverty both at an individual and corporate level.

Businesses lose value when the market value of their transformed assets is less than the sum of all ingredients (inputs) needed to produce goods or services. The value of those inputs minus the market value of the created or finished goods will result in a deficiency that makes shareholders, the government, and other stakeholders poorer than before any transactions took place. In that sense, society loses value and poverty is created.

Factors that can cause such a deficiency include excess capacity, lack of funding or overfunding, a poor market, and a poor environment for business growth, among many others. But none of these factors add up to a business that doesn't adapt to customer needs and preferences. Such a business will eventually die no matter how much money an entrepreneur throws at it. Whether a combination of these factors or a focus on one such as lack of meeting customer needs, deficiency occurs that leads to shrinking value and growing poverty.

CREATING POVERTY

Poverty results when deficiencies occur. Let's say a business spends $1 per bottle on lemons, sugar, water, and marketing costs to make and sell a bottle of lemonade, yet sells it for $.75 cents per bottle.

That business loses $.25 cents for each bottle sold. The more bottles of lemonade sold at a 25-cent loss, the bigger the loss that occurs. The business could sell 100 bottles and lose $250; but if that business sells 1 million bottles it loses $250,000. That's a lot of loss for the business and society. Imagine if millions of businesses operated with that kind of loss. Society will certainly become poorer as the businesses struggle, pay employees less, cut health coverage, or go under completely.

As a business struggles, it loses value and begins depleting assets to pay back loans, keep machinery running, and even pay workers. It may begin to liquidate machinery and other assets and begin to lay off workers, its most valuable asset. Too often a struggling business cuts its workforce which, while seeming to save money by not having to pay salaries, also causes asset depletion in the form of lost experience, training, and expertise. It also pushes additional workers into the overall labor market which, in turn, causes a decrease in salary for labor as workers saturate the market.

Downsizing—while sometimes caused by an increase in efficiency so fewer workers are needed—is often the result of internal and external factors pushing the business into crisis. When workers are cut, those workers receive no salary and cannot meet their needs, thus generating poverty when they are not able to sustain themselves.

Abject poverty, or extreme poverty, occurs when people have trouble meeting their most basic needs for food, clean water, shelter, sanitation, and health care. Haiti has 59 percent of its population living below the national poverty line, and 24 percent falling below the national extreme poverty line.[240] More than half the population of Somalia lives in poverty.[241] In the United States, the percentage of those living in poverty in 2016 was 12.7 percent. Almost 1 in 5 children live in poverty, with 6.7 percent of the population living in deep poverty in the U.S.[242]

According to the World Bank, whose mission statement is "Our Dream is a World Free of Poverty," much has been done worldwide to reduce poverty, but "the number of people living in extreme poverty globally remains unacceptably high."[243] The World Banks also says that reaching those in dire straits is difficult because they often live in remote areas in insecure countries. Yet abject poverty occurs in every country at some level. As those facing poverty try to survive, their needs clearly outstrip their income. Instead of finding ways to generate wealth, this population is just trying to survive. They are generating poverty day by day as their needs far outweigh their income.

Those in lesser degrees of need can also generate poverty when they struggle with adequate health and dental care, face occasional food insecurity, and can't pay bills on time or in full. All levels of poverty are a deficiency.

There are several theories about the reasons for poverty. First is the theory that culture creates poverty; that is, a culture of corruption, racism, or segregation is behind poverty creation. A second theory puts the onus on biology or the individual. A person's choices contribute to his or her level of poverty. If only they worked harder, they'd pull themselves out of poverty.[244]

Our job in this book is not to offer solutions to poverty or debate its causes, but instead to help countries avoid poverty. Whichever definition of deficiency you agree with and whatever reasons you believe poverty occurs, the bottom line is that basic needs are not met because income is not generated at needed levels. In my opinion, three top poverty accelerators—things that exacerbate poverty—are corruption, political instability, and foreign aid.

Poverty Creation

Poverty Accelerators

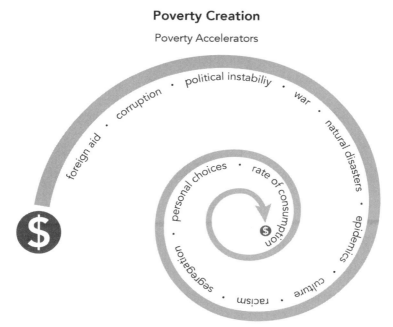

There are other poverty accelerators to be sure. Natural disasters such as hurricanes, earthquakes, tsunamis, and wildfires can devastate a city, a region, and even a country. Haiti's economy was nearly ruined by the 2010 earthquake, with over $12 billion lost in cumulative GDP as houses, roads, buildings, businesses, and stock were a total loss. Houston, Texas, and New Orleans, Louisiana, have faced huge losses caused by hurricanes. Wildfires in California have destroyed entire towns. Tsunamis in Bangladesh and Japan have caused widespread damage. Some people in these stricken areas have never recovered, with some relocating elsewhere or still struggling years later, thus accumulating poverty for the region on top of the losses created by natural disasters.

Other accelerators include war and epidemics. Consider the Ebola epidemics in Sierra Leone, Liberia, and Guinea that have killed thousands and continue to affect those and other countries, or AIDS epidemics, SARS outbreaks, and influenza outbreaks. These types of disasters can deplete a country's resources as they care for victims and try to curb and prevent additional outbreaks. Victims and families are thrown into chaos, with wages lost and workers lost to disease.

War, too, devastates countries and economies. Think of Syria, with hundreds of thousands dead and millions fleeing the country as refugees. The once-vibrant country now faces loss of people and the assets they represent, but also loss of property, infrastructure, trade, and even worldwide goodwill. As you can see, war, epidemics, and natural disasters can be poverty creators and poverty accelerators at the same time.

My book *From Aid to Trade* highlighted the pitfalls of an economy too dependent on foreign aid. That aid, while supplying needs in the short run, didn't allow for individuals and businesses to generate meaningful transactions and, thus, wealth. Countries with high foreign aid, high levels of corruption, and political upheaval create the perfect environment for poverty creation and are likely to have a majority of the population without enough income to meet their needs. Think of it as living in a swamp, a breeding ground for mosquitoes. If you live in or near that swamp, don't be surprised if you get malaria. If a country has high foreign aid, corruption, and political upheaval, don't be surprised that poverty is high.

Haiti is third in the world for experiencing natural disasters, but it is also well known for its corruption. One recent scandal involves Petrocaribe, an alliance of countries that made deals with Venezuela and its former president Hugo Chavez. Venezuela provided oil to Haiti and other countries to sell, with generous payback terms for the countries involved. However, corrupt officials in Haiti pocketed most of the money gained from oil sales, leaving no money to pay back Venezuela.

Now Haiti pays 15 percent of its national income to Venezuela while corrupt officials keep the money they stole. Instead of investing that money in services, infrastructure, and technology, Haiti is losing money thanks to corruption.

Not investing in improvements means moving backward for a society that cannot afford to help build into its citizens' well-being. Corruption can also prevent investors from offering loans at reasonable rates; in fact, investors increase the price of capital and other financial accelerators because of the increased risk of loss due to corruption. Instead of taking advantage of accelerators such as FDI and loans, among others, businesses and countries are falling prey to the poverty accelerators of corruption and political upheaval.

We have experienced the results of political instability in Haiti. Riots protesting a rise in fuel prices had people roaming the streets and damaging businesses, as well as preventing people who live day-to-day from trading their goods at the market for money or food. Because they couldn't go to market to sell and trade, opportunities for transactions were lost. Not only was trading lost, but fruit rotted, fish went bad, and sometimes goods stored in market stalls were stolen. Small businesses also experienced these losses.

The missed opportunity to sell for two or three days created an actual loss of goods and sales, but also accrued more loss in destruction of assets. This caused prices to rise to allow vendors to recoup their losses, which exacerbates poverty because incomes don't rise. And, once again, the deficiency widens.

On a personal level, my family and I planned to visit the south of the country for several days. We booked a hotel for three nights and planned to buy food at restaurants. We figured we'd spend at least $1,500 for our time away. But because of recent riots, we had to cancel our trip. The hotel didn't make a transaction for the room we would rent and the restaurants didn't make transactions for the food we would have eaten. We probably weren't the only ones who canceled our plans due to the instability, which caused businesses to miss out on transactions that, instead of creating wealth, contributed to poverty acceleration.

Haiti has also experienced many different presidents and interim presidents over the last decade or so. The democratic process is a huge struggle here, and the peaceful transition of power is not guaranteed. The political chaos has contributed to negative economic growth. The GDP annual growth rate rose from 0.8 in 2008 to 3.0 in 2009 before falling to –5.5 in 2010, the year of the earthquake. While GDP rose dramatically in 2011, it has fallen from that high of 5.5 to 1.2 in 2017.[245] The GDP per capita has remained almost the same in Haiti for years—at about $729 USD—a number only $28 higher than in 2008.[246] In ten years, Haiti's GDP per capita has risen just under $30. Political upheaval and corruption play a part in that sluggish growth, which is undermined further as Haiti's population grows.

Haiti's gross domestic product (the total finished products available) was valued at $8.40 billion in 2018. Per person that equals about $729, a change from $700 from the 1960s. Only thirty more dollars have been added to the GDP per capita in the last 50 years![247] Other countries that started at about $700 in the 1960s have added up to $6,000 worth of value. When the $729 is divided by 365 days, it comes out to be $1.99 on average per day worth of products per capita for the entire economy. This simply means that Haitians were still living in extreme poverty in 2018.[248]

Extreme poverty, as we define it today, has been reduced across the world from 36 percent to less than 9 percent since 2000. By the year 2050, 50 percent of the population living in extreme poverty will live in only two countries: Nigeria and Republic Democratic of Congo, both in Africa.[249] Extreme poverty is no longer a problem around the world, unless you live in countries like Haiti and Congo. Wealth creation is no longer an issue for most countries around the world today.

Another trait common to Haiti and other countries that produce fewer resources and wealth is their consumption level. The population increases faster than their wealth creation. It's like adding $10 to the $20 already in the bank, but withdrawing $35. The net result is negative $5, which is like spending $5 more than you have. This discrepancy is called poverty creation. When the population grew in Haiti at 1.31 percent in 2018, the GDP per capita grew at 1.5 percent, a net positive.[250] But when compared over, say, ten years, the rate of population growth far outpaces the rate of growth of the economy. This discrepancy creates poverty and puts upward pressure on the resources available per person.

In nominal terms, I calculated that Haitians gave birth to 152,210 more Haitians in 2018 at the same time GDP growth was, also on nominal terms, at $126 million. This translates to about $828 per year per capita, which is about $2.20 a day, a grossly insufficient amount to sustain anyone financially by any standard. It is a very small increase in GDP growth per capita, considering it went from 1.2 percent to 1.5 percent and is still peanuts compare to the need.

Let's agree, for argument's sake, that the minimum wage set by the government at $5.50 per day is sufficient (though we know it isn't) for the average Haitian. This would mean that the average Haitian is netting a deficiency of $3.30 a day, thus causing them to live in poverty by a greater amount than they actually bring in. They have more unfulfilled needs than they have satisfied ones. In simple terms, most Haitians are living in abject poverty and are creating more poverty by the day.

The problem of Haiti is not fancy economic indicators, barriers to entry, the diaspora, or fancy graphs shown by nonproductive NGO executives to raise more money. It is simply that we have more mouths than food, bodies than clothes, and feet than shoes. A lot of the symptoms we see daily are the products of a much more fundamental cause that is not so obvious: resources available are not enough for the number of people living here, and we Haitians are not taking any concrete steps to create more resources. That's the real root of the problem.

LEVELS OF POVERTY CREATION

Poverty creation has many aspects and many levels. Sometimes poverty creation is temporary for individuals and businesses; other times it is permanent. Here are a few of the creators of temporary or permanent poverty that can apply to both individuals and businesses.

Levels of Poverty Creation

1. Businesses and individuals that are investing in the future. Think of a college student who is accruing debt as he or she pays for school, but whose schooling is building earning potential for later. Or a business that is incurring temporary losses as it invests in new machinery or employee training. These entities are learning and gaining experience now to narrow the poverty gap in the future, though creating temporary poverty.

2. People or businesses that have invested in training or improvements but that are unable to meet their expenses. This might be a history major with college debt who is employed driving a truck, or a store that redecorated and added a new line of merchandise hoping to draw sales but whose customers haven't materialized. These entities have assets, but haven't found a way to use those assets to create balanced, much less superior, transactions.

3. People who have no skills or no ability (or desire) to learn skills needed to create earning potential. In developed countries, these folks aren't getting additional education, not

participating in apprenticeships, not looking for ways to increase earnings. In developing countries, these people may not finish high school and may work on farms or at other low-paying jobs. They don't have assets to transform; they live in a constant state of starting from zero. They may never have had an opportunity for education, which puts them much further behind in acquiring intangible assets that allow them to narrow the gap of poverty.

4. People and businesses with assets but that fall prey to outside events. Individuals may fall prey to addictions, mental illness, or life traumas not properly addressed. Businesses may falter due to devastating natural disasters, a toppling economy, or even thievery. Asset recovery and growth become impossible.

Poverty creation is nuanced and has many contributing factors, with each country experiencing different factors at different times. The bottom line, however, is that the poverty each country creates looks much the same: individuals and businesses don't earn enough to meet their needs.

We have discussed in previous chapters how countries can transform sector assets into superior transactions and wealth creation, but those same countries can also turn assets into poverty creation. Assets can be untapped and untransformed, creating no wealth and no value added.

Agricultural land can sit unused or overused, providing either no crops at all or diminished returns from land that is depleted. The Manufacturing sector can founder by not taking advantage of value chain opportunities. Services can miss out when technology lags behind, not providing businesses and individuals full access to digital resources. The Tourism sector doesn't contribute when historical or cultural sites are undeveloped and/or inaccessible. Instead of becoming assets to the overall economy, undeveloped sectors become liabilities. The liabilities are huge, as each one prevents job creation and superior transactions that lead to wealth creation at individual and national levels.

We've also demonstrated the relationship between assets, sector growth, and national growth, and how the OBED study verified the link between them. If those assets aren't transformed through transactions, individual and country-wide wealth does not accrue or does not accrue at a fast-enough rate. Resources that are left untapped or don't grow as a country's needs are growing can be creating poverty.

Any country not creating enough wealth is creating poverty instead. An individual not earning enough to meet his or her needs is creating poverty. This is a substantial concept to grasp, yet is quite simple: poverty is essentially an unmet need because of lack of sufficient income.

Just as people learn how to create wealth by learning skills and putting those skills into practice, people can learn how to create poverty as well. Some become quite good at it. Creating wealth implies knowledge of how accelerators work and using those accelerators to turn assets and liabilities into opportunities. In the same way, poverty can be learned and its accelerators can be used to create and continue a cycle of poverty that can be worsened by political instability, corruption, and foreign aid.

LEADERS HAVE RESPONSIBILITIES

A country's leaders have a responsibility to bring everything they need together to create wealth, not poverty. The country of Rwanda, whose history is marked by the 1994 genocide, is on the road to economic recovery. Rwanda was ranked tenth on the World Bank's list of Top 10 Improvers for 2017/18.[251] This index both tracks and inspires countries to make reforms to help small and medium businesses, as well as entrepreneurs, grow and create wealth through job creation and investment.[252]

Rwanda is a top reformer in the history of the Doing Business Index, thanks to the government purposefully creating an environment that allows businesses to thrive and investments to pay off. "Rwanda has adopted a very bold and ambitious approach to reforming its business environment," said Louise Kanyonga, head of the Rwanda Development Board's Strategy and Competitiveness Department.[253]

Key areas of reform include ease of registering property, starting a business, getting credit, and paying taxes.[254] Private investments are up 60 percent and FDI is up almost 40 percent in the last eight years, said Kanyonga.[255] The poverty rate dropped significantly in just a four-year span (2011–2014), from 44 percent to 39 percent.[256]

Rwanda's GDP made slow growth since 1960, finally hitting the billion-dollar mark in 1979. That growth reached nearly $2 billion in 1993, then dropped significantly in 1994. It reached $2 billion again in 2004, and between then and 2017 has grown to just over $9 billion.[257] Clearly Rwanda's purposeful inducements to help businesses has paid off in rising GDP. The GNI PPP rose from $620 in 2000 to $1,330 in 2010 to $1,990 in 2017.[258]

Compare the growth of Rwanda with the decline of Syria. Since the conflict began in 2011, Syria's economy has fallen by more than 70 percent.[259] Contributing factors include huge infrastructure damage, lower domestic production, and high inflation, among other things.[260] The ongoing conflict has worsened the humanitarian crisis, with more than 13 million in need inside the country and the number of registered refugees rising to more than 5 million.[261]

GDP was at $61.9 billion in 2013, and by 2015 had shrunk to $50.2 billion. GDP per capita (PPP) shrunk from $3,300 in 2014 to $2,900 in 2015, the last year statistics were recorded.[262] Economic forecasts say that GDP annual growth rate will fall throughout 2019, and GDP per capita will fall as well.[263] Forecasters also say that GDP per capita PPP will fall dramatically throughout 2019.[264]

While there is no way to predict when the Syrian war will end or what specific economic effects will occur, it is easy to see that political upheaval and war can turn an economy such as Syria's upside down. Citizens are displaced within and outside the country, transactions are disrupted by war, and businesses (and people) struggle to survive.

CONCLUSION

Any country, business, and citizen not creating wealth is creating poverty. When transactions are left on the table, when assets are not leveraged, when accelerators are unused, the result is not only a lack of wealth but a growth in poverty. To help prevent growth in poverty, a country's leaders have a responsibility to create an environment conducive to wealth creation. Thanks to our OBED study and as outlined in previous chapters, we know that environment must include pro-business policies, access to financial accelerators, appropriate development of assets, education and health, infrastructure development, and a ready labor pool.

We also know that the opposite of that healthy environment—political instability, corruption, and foreign aid—can lead to poverty. Countries must find ways to move away from poverty creators and develop wealth creators instead.

Economist Adam Smith talked about one side of the equation—how the wealth of one person creates the wealth of a nation. His "invisible hand" theory showed how individuals each accumulating wealth helped create the wealth of the whole nation. But what if that theory also works the other way? What if individuals, each creating poverty, contribute to the poverty of the nation? It's the "invisible hand" principle in reverse.

During the recession in 2008, many people lost jobs and couldn't make their mortgage payments. They owed more on their homes that those homes were worth in the faltering housing market, with many of those underwater homes lost to foreclosure. One by one, house by house, the economy suffered more and more. The reverse "invisible hand" worked in the area of loss. The housing market wasn't the only trouble area during the recession, but it is an example of how loss piling on loss hurt an economy.

The negative effect of creating poverty has just as much impact on society as the positive effects of creating wealth. While we can't go into depth on those negative effects here, nor the reasons behind poverty creation, the lesson is that people can become efficient at creating poverty. If they have lived in poverty their whole lives, they become adept at staying in that poverty. If people have spent their lives creating wealth or watching other people do it, they become adept at creating wealth themselves.

Luc in Haiti lives on less that $2 a day and has done so for years. He can envision a different future for himself, but doesn't know how to get there. John in the U.S. makes minimum wage and lives in poverty, yet dreams of creating a better life through education. Which one has a better chance of moving from poverty creation to wealth creation? John does; he can get college loans, qualify for government assistance, participate in job training workshops, and get help creating a resumé. Luc, on the other hand, needs so many more resources to climb out of the pit of poverty. Haiti doesn't have government assistance programs, loans for college are almost unheard of, and job training workshops are rare.

Both men live in poverty, but one has a much better chance of rising out of poverty thanks to the programs and stability his country offers. One will likely struggle his entire life, unable to access the accelerators John can. Luc continues to create poverty, as will most of his fellow Haitians. As the individual goes, so goes the country.

From an OBED point of view, poverty is prevalent and is the result of unbalanced transactions and deficiencies, regardless of the reasons why. The more poverty that is created, the easier it is to keep creating poverty. That poverty creation starts with individuals and migrates to sectors and the whole economy.

The OBED principles of using assets and liabilities to create superior transactions and Smith's principle of the "invisible hand" can work positively—creating wealth—and negatively by creating poverty. My dream for developing economies is to step away from creating poverty and into creating wealth.

9

PROGRESS AND REGRESS: THE OBED PRINCIPLES APPLIED TO TEN COUNTRIES

This book focuses on OBED principles, particularly wealth creation, offering examples of countries and businesses that put those principles to work. Now we want to offer five examples of countries that have been putting some of the OBED principles into action and making progress. We'll also look at five countries that are poorer than they were even five to ten years ago. Some had been considered rich but have moved backward economically, and others were poor to begin with and are now poorer still. These countries have not practiced OBED theory enough or at all and have suffered for it.

Our examples range from big countries such as Venezuela to small ones such as Nauru, from Europe to South America to the Middle East. None of the countries are perfect and, in fact, many face deep and pervasive struggles. Yet each example offers instruction on how to apply, or not apply, OBED principles.

OBED POSITIVE COUNTRIES

OBED positive countries intentionally practice at least three of the OBED principles discussed in this book. As we've shown, countries don't have to practice all of the principles to be OBED positive, and there may be other principles not mentioned in this book that have yielded great results. But what we have found is that countries that transform their assets and liabilities into marketable opportunities via OBED principles can change the lives of millions.

REPUBLIC OF NAURU

This tiny island nation located northeast of Australia has a population of about 11,000 and a land area of 21 square kilometers. The coral atoll is close enough to Australia to benefit from the larger country's economy. Phosphate mining and exporting, which began in the early 1900s, gained new life in the mid-2000s and has been a huge boost to Nauru's economy.[265] It has seen an average 16 percent GDP growth over the last 10 years.[266]

Nauru has practiced OBED principle Number 5 by turning assets into transactions via its phosphate deposits. Primary phosphate reserves had been exhausted, but mining "secondary phosphate" began in 2007.[267] Phosphate is 75 percent of Nauru's exports yearly, shipping primarily to Australia, New Zealand, and parts of Asia.[268]

As Nauru considers next steps, one liability may become an asset and begin to create transactions (OBED Principle 5). The limestone stacks left over after phosphate mining could be mined for dolomite, which could be exported and thus create profit.[269] Also, the United Arab Emirates invested in a solar energy plant. Nauru is looking for FDI to develop these and other industries.[270]

The country also has a small manufacturing sector that centers mostly on coconut products. Nauru is working on growing this sector, which coincides with OBED Principle 2 that encourages countries to diversify in all sectors. It may be easier for Nauru to depend solely on mining to create wealth, but diversifying into Manufacturing allows it to grow wealth in other sectors as well. OBED-practicing countries make a point to diversify as Nauru is attempting to do.

Nauru has taken advantage of another asset—proximity to Australia—to create transactions. The Australian Regional Processing Center for those seeking asylum in Australia opened in Nauru in 2012, and has generated income for the government and individuals who are employed there. The government also generates revenue from payments for fishing licenses, while the fishermen generate transactions thanks to the ocean, one of the biggest natural assets ever.[271]

Nauru has again practiced OBED Principle 5 by turning assets—proximity to Australia and the surrounding ocean—into transactions. OBED Principle 4 also comes into play as growth in sectors and businesses benefits society as a whole. The jobs created by the processing center (as controversial as it is in the media) allow workers to gain an income, which they inject into the island's small businesses as they purchase food, goods, and services. The same can be said for the fishing industry that provides resources and goods for trade; fish markets, boat repair shops, fish processing businesses, etc., all benefit, which helps create a more stable and growing society. Society benefits as individuals and businesses benefit.

GDP per capita in Nauru rose from $11,600 in 2015 to $12,300 in 2017. Overall GDP rose from $139.4 million in 2015 to $160 million in 2017.[272] Unemployment was estimated at 90 percent in 2004 and 23 percent in 2011.[273]

While Nauru remains heavily dependent on Australia for economic aid and imports from Australia make up 67.5 percent of all imports,[274] the small island nation is building a manufacturing base and looking to the future. It has many problems to overcome including environmental woes and corruption, but the nation is applying the OBED principle of turning assets into transactions to create wealth. Those principles it has put into action have yielded results.

While the country is making visible progress in many economic indicators, Nauru remains a country with limited diversification in investments, markets, job creation, and overall business opportunities. Its leadership needs to remain deliberate in looking for more Industry and Service sector opportunities, particularly in technology, to further create superior transactions so even more wealth can be created.

FINLAND

Finland was one of the first countries to get a loan from the World Bank Group to help rebuild its economy after World War II ravaged the European continent. Since then Finland has worked with the World Bank, along with other member governments, to help finance and create programs to help eradicate poverty in developing nations.[275]

This small Scandinavian country has seen its GDP skyrocket from $5.9 billion (USD) in 1960 to a high of $283.7 billion in 2008. The global financial crisis of 2008–2009 caused slippage in GDP ($232.4 billion in 2015), but by 2017 GDP had risen to $251.8 billion.[276]

Poverty rates don't even show up on World Bank data charts.[277] GDP per capita is $46,016 (USD),[278] one of the highest in the world. Finland is ranked 11th out of 140 in the Global Competitive Index, where it ranked first (with other countries) in macroeconomic stability (Pillar 4) and first in the Skills (Pillar 6) subcategory of mean years of schooling. It also ranked first in soundness of its banks (Pillar 9, Financial system) and third overall in Pillar 9.[279] Forbes listed it at #13 in its "Best Countries for Business" list.[280]

Because of its cold climate, Finland has never had a huge agriculture component but does grow basic staples, and its Forestry sector is important. Its Manufacturing sector, however, is robust and focuses on wood, metals, engineering, telecommunications, and electronics industries.[281] The country also is a big promoter of startup companies focused on information and communications technology, gaming, cleantech, and biotech.[282]

Finland has practiced OBED Principle 1 of moving the largest share of investment, GDP, and job creation from Agriculture to Manufacturing (or Industry) to Services to create growth, wealth, and jobs. In 2007, 4.5 percent of jobs were in Agriculture, 25.7 percent in Industry, and 69.7 percent in Services. By 2017, Service sector jobs jumped to 73.8 percent, Industry jobs fell to 22.2 percent, and Agriculture to 3.8 percent.[283]

The country's percentage of GDP from these sectors, in the third quarter of 2018, was as follows: 1339 EUR Million from Agriculture, 7937 EUR Million from Manufacturing, and 29,718 EUR Million from Services.[284] Health and social services were the biggest employers in the Service sector, along with wholesale and retail trade. Almost 40 percent of Service jobs were in the public sector, with accommodations, catering, transport and storage, and information and communications jobs also vital to the sector.[285]

Finland has been on a positive trajectory since World War II ended, thanks in part to practicing OBED principles. The country moved from Agriculture to Manufacturing to Services (Principle 1), increasing GDP and PPP almost yearly. It also diversified its manufacturing and exports, years ago moving away from wool and cotton because of competition from low-wage countries specializing in low-cost textile manufacturing.[286] Electronics is now the largest manufacturing industry (25 percent share), with Nokia the largest producer of mobile phones. Paper production is another top product, though Finland faces competition from Asia and South America.[287] The Services sector also remains high at 72.7 percent.[288]

Finland, particularly post WWII and in the 1980s, exercised OBED Principle 2 by diversifying its Manufacturing sector to meet international needs and moving into the Services sector. The country has made pro-business decisions, put pro-business policies in place, and exemplifies the economic prosperity that comes as a result of following OBED principles.

BOTSWANA

Botswana, located in the center of southern Africa, gained its independence from Britain in 1966. At that time it was one of the world's poorest nations, but now it is one of the developing world's successes.[289] Diamond mining, a concerted fight against corruption, investment in education, and good economic policy has moved the country from poor to upper-middle income.[290]

The country's economy has averaged 5 percent growth for the past decade, driven by mining, construction, Service sector growth, and public investment.[291] The ruling Botswana Democratic Party has offered steady leadership, with fiscal spending focused on ending poverty, inclusive growth, and job creation.[292]

Botswana has benefited greatly from transforming its asset—diamonds—into meaningful transactions that yield wealth. OBED Principle 5 is hard at work, with the country one of the world's top three diamond producers (behind Russian and Canada).[293] Botswana produced almost 23 million carats of diamonds in 2017, worth $3.3 billion.[294] The industry contributes 20 percent of the country's GDP, with 20 percent of the population employed in the diamond mining industry.[295] Prince Harry of Britain even sourced the diamond for Meghan Markle's engagement ring from Botswana, a country he has visited often in the last twenty years.[296]

Yet diamond mining won't last forever, said Minister of Environment Tshekedi Khama. "We have to go from relying on diamonds to diversifying the economy," he said.[297]

He is speaking right into OBED Principle 2, which says that healthy countries diversify into productive sectors. Botswana is diversifying in part by building up its tourism industry; 1.6 million visited the country in 2015, with that number growing. The sector yields about 140,000 jobs as tourists visit to catch glimpses of wildlife that can roam the streets; markets, hotels, and restaurants are popping up as well.[298] Botswana is practicing OBED Principle 5 as it takes its natural asset—wildlife—and turns it into transactions via the tourism industry.

One of Botswana's biggest projects is the Kazungula Bridge, which opens a transport corridor between Zambia and Botswana. The bridge is part of the overall plan to reduce transit time and facilitate increased trade between the two countries.[299] The project and the ease of trade between countries will also add to their global competitiveness. The African Development Bank helped fund the project,[300] and provides an example of how accelerators can be used to improve a nation's economy via transactions and the overall well-being of its people (OBED Principle 4).

The country has also made a concerted effort to fight the AIDS epidemic. In the early 2000s, AIDS threatened to decimate an adult population that had, at 25 percent, one of the highest infection rates in the world; by 2012, almost all citizens who needed AIDS drugs received them, and transmission of HIV from infected mothers to their babies was at just 4 percent, down from a high of 40 percent.[301]

The government, then under President Festus Mogae, made HIV/AIDS a top priority.[302] Through government spending, international donors, and research institutions, Botswana began to get a handle on the epidemic.[303] By doing so, Botswana improved the lives of its people overall and saved a generation or more of lives. People once condemned to death from AIDS can now, thanks to drugs and prevention education, contribute to society. The fight against AIDS/HIV improved society as a whole, thus putting into practice OBED Principle 4.

Botswana's economy also mirrors OBED Principle 1 in that just 1.8 percent of GDP comes from Agriculture, 27.5 percent from Industry, and 70.6 percent from the Services sector.[304] The country, once heavily based on subsistence agriculture, has moved the way all successful countries move: into dependence on Manufacturing and Service sectors to create wealth.

Botswana can benefit, however, from deepening their Manufacturing and Service sectors, encouraging innovation in these sectors, and developing more private-sector jobs. It struggles with income inequality and unemployment, but with continued emphasis on OBED Principle 3 (decreasing income inequality through educating the workforce) and Principle 2 (diversifying in all sectors), Botswana can create even more jobs and become even more economically successful.

GHANA

Ghana—once a country mired in civil strife, political unrest, and poverty—is well on its way to economic and political stability. The West African nation has held peaceful elections for several decades and is taking advantage of economic opportunities brought on by the discovery of offshore oil deposits.

The country's GDP rose consistently starting in 2000 when it was at $4.9 billion to $47.3 billion in 2017, with occasional small drops in some years. The nation's GDP was just $1.2 billion in 1960.[305]

Ghana has put key OBED principles into action. Principle 2 is seen in Ghana's investment in cocoa bean production. While OBED countries generally move from Agriculture to Manufacturing to Services, it's also an OBED positive to invest in sectors that promise the most growth, especially sectors that, when diversified, offer amplified transactions to create superior value added. Cocoa promises growth for Ghana's Agriculture sector.

Niche Cocoa is located in a suburb of Accra and produces cocoa liquor, cocoa butter, and cocoa cake to be used around the world in the food industry, as well as a wide variety of chocolate bars and other products for retail sale.[306] Niche calls itself "Ghana's leading bean-to-bar producer."[307]

Rather than simply harvesting the cocoa beans and exporting them, Niche Cocoa has taken advantage of the value chain to create even more transactions. The factory, located in Tema's Free Zone Enclave outside Accra, has a capacity of 60,000 tons per year and uses top-quality equipment to produce its many products.[308] The move into the confectionary market is recent, allowing the company to not only ship products abroad but to take advantage of the domestic market for chocolate bars, spreads, and instant drinks.[309]

It's easy to see how Niche Cocoa has used accelerators such as pro-business policies, Tema's Free Zone Enclave, loans to purchase top-grade machinery, training and education to create a dependable workforce, and other accelerators in the financial sector to create a vital business that contributes to the economy.

As we know from OBED Principle 4, as go the businesses, so goes society. Niche Cocoa is doing its part by creating hundreds of good-paying, skilled jobs, with plans to hire more.[310] Those workers contribute to the local economy by paying taxes, purchasing goods and services, and enrolling their children in school. Other cocoa-processing companies are doing the same.

Principle 5 comes into play as the country located along the Atlantic Ocean has turned its asset of oil deposits into meaningful transactions. Tullow Oil, based in the United Kingdom, and Eni, based in Italy, both expanded their operations in Ghana,[311] with oil production on the rise. Ghana's President Nana Akufo-Adda expected an 8.3 percent growth in the economy in 2018, up from the 6.8 percent initially forecast.[312]

Ghana can gain much economic benefit if it can provide equipment and services to help support these international companies, thus inserting itself into the value chain. The government has mandated minimum levels of participation by local companies, with some sectors requiring at least 10 percent of equity held by Ghanaian businesses.[313] Despite the mandates, Ghanaian firms need FDI to allow them to partner with businesses that can contribute knowledge and technology to help the process[314] and thus help the Ghanaian economy.

Growth in Ghana's Service sector in the last decades highlights OBED Principle 1, which states that countries generally move from Agriculture to Industry to Services on their paths to wealth and growth. Its Service sector is on a growth trajectory, with 29.5 percent of jobs in the Service sector in 1991 and just over 45 percent of jobs in the sector in 2017.[315] While the sector is growing, the Industry sector with oil production and Agriculture with cocoa beans are heavy influences in the job market. Hopefully Ghana will begin to move to even more jobs in the Service sector in the next decades.

Ghana is one of the fastest-growing economies in the world, according to the *New York Times* article cited above. It has taken advantage of its assets, focused on the sectors that promise the most growth, and has grown its Service sector. While its troubles aren't over—the unemployment rate increased from 4 percent to 5.8 percent from 2011 to 2017, with youth unemployment as high as 11.5 percent[316]—Ghana is making strides toward becoming a successful, wealthy nation.

MALAYSIA

Malaysia comprises the lower Malay Peninsula, with the exception of Singapore, and Sabah and Sarawak on the northern coast of Borneo. The South China Sea divides the regions of this country that has made concerted efforts to diversify its economy.[317] By moving from primarily a producer of raw materials for export to wider Manufacturing and Services sectors, Malaysia has seen much growth.

GDP rose from $845.6 billion in 2015 to $933.3 billion in 2017, with GDP per capita rising from $27,100 in 2015 to $29,100 in 2017.[318] In good OBED fashion, Malaysia has exemplified Principle 1 as it moved from Agriculture (8.8 percent of GDP in 2017) to Industry (37.6 percent) to Services (53.6 percent).[319]

It has added to the value chain as well. Agriculture products include palm oil, rubber, and timber, among others. Industries include rubber and palm oil processing and manufacturing, and timber processing. Industry also includes petroleum and natural gas production, as well as pharmaceuticals, medical technology, electronics, and semiconductors.[320] Tourism continues to draw visitors and their money as well.

Malaysia has also tapped into accelerators such as FDI, which increased by 250 percent in the first three quarters of 2018 to $11.8 billion USD, according to the country's finance minister.[321] One of the country's long-term economic goals is to move the Manufacturing sector from simply assembling imported parts to designing and producing original products.[322] Malaysia will put priority on automated manufacturing, biotech, microelectronics/IT, and energy tech.[323]

Malaysia's Ministry of Finance predicts a 5.9 percent growth in the Services sector in 2019, with the information and communication subsector growth expected at 8 percent, along with food and beverage and accommodation subsector growth projected at 6.9 percent.[324] Also expecting growth are wholesale and retail trade (along with e-commerce), and finance and insurance.[325]

OBED principles are all over Malaysia's vibrant economy. Principle 1 is exhibited in the move from Agriculture to Manufacturing in the last decades, and the push to grow the Services sector. Principle 2 is manifest in Malaysia's investment in sectors that promise the most growth. Manufacturing is one example, as the country steps into creating goods for export (palm oil, timber, rubber products) and develops its electronics manufacturing.

Principle 3—the idea that income inequality can be created and must be acknowledged and worked on—is also seen in Malaysia. The income gap between the richest and poorest in Malaysia still needs work, though the Gini coefficient has dropped from 0.513 in 1970 to 0.399 in 2016.[326] A recent study calls for investment in human capital—improving education quality in particular—to continue to lower income inequality.[327]

Principles 4 and 5 are evident as well, as Malaysia continues to turn its assets—timber, gas and oil deposits, human capital, palm oil, etc.—into superior transactions. Additional assets such as proximity to China, Indonesia, and other nations are translated into trade opportunities. All of these transactions benefit society as a whole as the nation gains more wealth and works to increase that wealth and ensure that all of its citizens benefit.

OBED NEGATIVE COUNTRIES

While some countries are deep into using methods and assets to help their economies, many countries have serious trouble putting OBED principles into place. They have trouble generating basic economic value added, let alone generate superior economic value added. They suffer greatly, as do their people. We include their stories as well.

SOUTH SUDAN

South Sudan, which separated from Sudan in 2011 after decades of civil war, remains rocked by war as factions within the new country fight for power. The country remains heavily dependent on humanitarian assistance, with 90 percent of food, capital, and services imported from neighbors such as Uganda, Kenya, and Sudan.[328]

GDP has dropped from $24.52 billion in 2015 to $20.01 billion in 2017, with GDP per capita falling from $2,100 in 2015 to $1,600 in 2017.[329] Sixty-six percent of the population is below the poverty line[330] and living on less than about $2 a day, up from 50.6 percent in 2009.[331]

South Sudan struggles mightily with high levels of government corruption, little infrastructure, famine, and huge displacement of the population.[332]

Yet this land-locked country is not without resources. It has one of the best agricultural areas on the African continent, with fertile soil and plenty of water. South Sudan also produced more than half of the former Sudan's total oil output.[333]

South Sudan, due to war and corruption, hasn't been able to turn its assets into transactions and increased wealth. Farmland sits fallow and oil production is hurt by war. Its people are displaced and starving. Those three assets alone—arable land, oil production, and human capital—could likely turn this country around should those assets be turned into transactions instead of going to waste.

By applying OBED principles, particularly the principle that simply having assets doesn't guarantee economic transformation until those assets become transactions, South Sudan can begin to move forward. Yet that forward motion can only occur when corruption, war, and foreign aid are overcome.

GREECE

Greece, a country hit by financial earthquakes in recent years, is ranked #42 on 2018's Doing Business, World Bank Forbes' "Best Countries for Doing Business," with a 1.4 percent GDP growth rate, a GDP per capita of $18,600, and trade balance/GDP of –0.8 percent.[334] Its Gini coefficient, a measurement of wealth distribution with lower numbers better, rose from a low of .33.6 in 2009 to .36.2 in 2012, with 2015 at .36.[335]

There are numerous explanations for Greece's financial downfall, which included the 2015 default on its debt payment to the International Monetary Fund to the tune of 1.6 billion EUR. It was the first time a developed country missed a payment of this size.[336] Some blame Greece's joining the Eurozone, but others argue that Greece's economy was struggling long before 2001. In fact, the government admits that it doctored budget figures to be allowed into the Eurozone, with the hope that joining would help the economy.[337] At the heart of the issue is understanding why Greece had that much debt to begin with.

The real issue, according to Investopedia author Matthew Johnston, "stems from a lack of revenue" and that lack of revenue "is the result of systematic tax evasion."[338] This evasion—under-reporting income and over-reporting debt—was "more of a social norm, one that wasn't remedied in time."[339] The results were catastrophic, with small and medium businesses struggling, the Greek government borrowing cheaply what it couldn't repay, and austerity measures that Greeks hated.[340] Lack of tax revenue in OBED terms is symptomatic of a lack of transactions within the economy, meaning not enough assets are being turned into marketable opportunities that yield tax revenue.

With the global recession of 2007, Greece's deficit worsened as tax revenues, already low, sank lower. Capital began to dry up and a bailout was needed,[341] with conditions set that included austerity measures which served only to create a vicious cycle of deeper recession and subsequent unemployment, which reached 25.4 percent in August 2012.[342]

OBED Principle 4 states that focusing on meaningful, market-based transactions brings superior returns as businesses generate wealth, which creates more opportunities and more resources that create value for the business and society as a whole. Greece, however, lacked the wherewithal to enforce paying taxes, and its leaders lied about budget numbers. Meaningful transactions cannot be made if the government hasn't created a climate that allows for use of accelerators to create business growth—through laws, policies, and enforcement.

Greece, in fact, helped create poverty with its lack of enforcement and appropriate fiscal policies. Unemployment was high, homelessness increased, suicides rose, and public health overall declined as health care become unaffordable or nonexistent.[343] In such a precarious environment, it is hard to apply OBED principles to their fullest with the use of accelerators; potential investors, both foreign and domestic, are wary of lack of return on investment. Lack of growth keeps tax revenue, jobs, and other economic indicators worsening month by month.

Greece is on a slow rise back to fiscal health, but much remains to be done. By putting into practice the OBED principles of focusing on meaningful, market-based transactions and creating a safe and honest climate, Greece may become healthier once again.

LIBYA

Libya has a history of occupation and unrest, with well-known strongman Colonel Muammar al-Qadhafi one of the most infamous. He assumed power in a military coup in 1969 and began promoting his brand of Islam. Qadhafi was behind the downing of two airliners and a bombing in Berlin,[344] which ultimately led to United Nations sanctions in 1992. The sanctions were lifted in 2003, after which he began normalizing relations with the West.[345]

But unrest across the region erupted in Libya in early 2011, causing Qadhafi to launch a brutal crackdown on protesters that led to civil war and UN intervention. His regime fell in mid-2011, leading to years of political maneuvering. In September 2017, the UN announced a new plan for reconciliation.[346]

Libya's economy is almost entirely dependent on oil and gas exports, which fluctuate with political instability, production disruptions, and global oil prices. Since 2014, Libya's currency has lost much of its value and inflation has risen. Power outages, access to clean drinking water, medical care, education, and safe housing have all declined.[347] While oil production has risen recently, it still hasn't reached pre-Revolution highs of over a million barrels a day.[348]

Libya has not capitalized on OBED Principle 1—moving the largest parts of their private investment, job creation, and GDP growth from Agriculture to Manufacturing to Services—in part because of its dependence on oil production. Agriculture makes up 1.3 percent of GDP, Manufacturing (Industry) at 52.3 percent, and Services at 46.4 percent.[349] Countries that move from poverty to wealth put emphasis on Services jobs, something Libya is lacking. While the country is diversified in some ways, it lacks the strong diversification that would yield more transactions and more wealth.

Inflation rates (consumer prices) rose from 25.9 percent in 2016 to 28.5 percent in 2017, with about a third of the population living at or below the national poverty line.[350] Unemployment is at about 19 percent, with youth unemployment at 48 percent and female unemployment at 25 percent, and 85 percent of the labor force employed in the public sector.[351] Public sector employment is one of the pitfalls in Libyan society; public sector, bureaucratic jobs sustained by the government's fluctuating oil revenue don't produce a growing economy indicative of OBED adherence. Private sector jobs create the best transactions, but these types of jobs and businesses are almost nonexistent in Libya.

Libya struggles with most of the OBED principles. The country hasn't diversified its economy (Principle 2), almost stubbornly remaining tied to oil production that fluctuates wildly. Also, with the majority of workers employed in the public sector instead of the private sector, the government is overburdened with paying those salaries and other benefits. Private sector jobs would likely yield better jobs and thus better transactions, but such jobs aren't there or Libya's workforce isn't qualified to fill them (Principle 3).

Clearly Libyan society is suffering due to political unrest and other influences. Businesses suffer as transactions are interrupted or stop altogether, with little or no investment (such as FDI) made in those businesses on a small or large scale. When businesses can't make transactions, the country as a whole suffers (Principle 4).

Libya may be making efforts to rebuild after years of war and sanctions. The most pressing needs—public services such as water and electricity—must be met first before economic issues such as diversification and increasing transactions can begin to increase wealth in this struggling nation.

VENEZUELA

The South American country of Venezuela has backslidden economically in recent years, in part because of its heavy dependence on revenue from oil, which accounts for a huge percentage of export revenue and almost half of all government revenue.[352] Oil production has declined, however, which is helping throw the country into a tailspin.

GDP has declined from an estimated $531 billion in 2015 to $381 billion in 2017, with GDP per capita declining from $17,300 in 2015 to $12,500 in 2017.[353] Add to this an inflation rate of about 2,000 percent and unemployment rates of nearly 30 percent,[354] and the country is in deep trouble.

Venezuela's heavy dependence on oil revenue goes against OBED Principle 2, which calls for diversification in all sectors to allow for increased transactions. When oil revenue falls, the Venezuelan economy also falls and the people suffer.

The Venezuelan government, first under Hugo Chavez and then under President Nicolas Maduro, has increased state control over the economy, instituting tight currency controls and price controls.[355] With private enterprises struggling to afford basics to keep the businesses running, fewer goods become available on the open market; what goods are available are strictly controlled by the government. This has led to a growing black market, corruption,[356] and citizens struggling to buy even a loaf of bread, much less needed medicines and other goods. Many are fleeing the country as they look for a better, more stable life.

Stories abound that highlight the cost of basic foods and necessities in Venezuela. The World Economic Forum posted a story that included photos from Reuters showing the stacks of cash needed to buy a roasting chicken, a roll of toilet paper, sanitary pads, and a kilogram of meat.[357] The Maduro government tried to curb hyperinflation by cutting five zeros from all prices and currency in August 2018, raising the minimum wage by 3,000 percent, tax increases, and tying key things such as salaries and prices to a state-backed cryptocurrency.[358] Economists around the world suggest that more chaos will follow.[359]

One Reuters's story states that another 2 million will leave Venezuela in 2019, raising the total number of refugees to 5.3 million.[360] Colombia, Brazil, Ecuador, and Peru have taken in the majority of the refugees.[361]

Government policies are clearly hurting the Venezuelan economy, and businesses are not making positive transactions and generating wealth. OBED Principle 4 is out the window as society suffers due to policies that breed hyperinflation, corruption, black market activity, and masses fleeing the country.

For Venezuela to get back on track economically, policies must change, dependence on oil revenue must be curbed, and citizens must once again be able to make transactions that create wealth. Obviously there are many more things that must change in Venezuela, but these suggestions, based on OBED principles, are a start.

YEMEN

Yemen's development as a country has been arrested by ongoing conflict. North Yemen gained its independence in 1918, with South Yemen coming into being when the British withdrew in 1967.[362] But a mass exodus from south to north three years later, fueled by the southern government leaning toward Marxist policies, prompted much hostility between the two states.[363]

The two countries unified in 1990 as the Republic of Yemen, with a brief civil war halted in 1994; by 2004 fighting resumed in the country, this time between the government and the Houthis, a Muslim minority.[364] Protesters rallied against President Salih in 2001, fed by high unemployment, a poor economy, and corruption. There were talks and resolutions made and yet more fighting, with no resolution in sight and North and South Yemen continuing to fight each other.[365]

The ongoing war has caused poverty and unemployment on a huge scale. Exports have all but halted, inflation has risen, and infrastructure has been severely damaged. It is estimated that more than 80 percent of the population needs humanitarian assistance.[366]

GDP has dropped from $90.6 billion in 2015 to $73.6 billion in 2017; GDP growth fell almost 17 percent in 2015 and almost 6 percent in 2017. GDP per capita has fallen from $3,200 in 2015 to $2,500 in 2017.[367]

This struggling country has a long way to go to reach stability and wealth despite assets such as oil and natural gas deposits, low-cost labor, deep water ports, access to the Gulf of Aden, and proximity to wealthy neighbors such as Saudi Arabia and Oman. It would do well to practice OBED Principle 1, that of moving from Agriculture to Industry to Services.

Currently Yemen's GDP is made up of 20.3 percent Agriculture, 11.8 percent Industry, and 67.9 percent in Services.[368] While the Service sector is a seemingly healthy one, Industry is well below what it should be, perhaps in part due to high infrastructure damage and corruption.

A recent Reuters article stated, "Yemen's tanking economy threatens to kill more people than bombs and guns." Food prices are on the rise and famine threatens millions, according to the story.[369]

It is clear that Yemen's economy can begin to improve only when political stability is restored. The war has done almost irreparable damage to its people, infrastructure, economy, and land. Accelerators such as FDI, loans, and equipment are almost nonexistent in a country on the brink of disaster. While Yemen must rely on foreign aid to mitigate the deaths of millions from starvation, overdependence on that aid in the future may hamper recovery attempts.

Yemen's leaders, both business and political, must seek ways to restore basic transactions, and hopefully superior ones, to restore the country to stability.

CONCLUSION

As you can see, countries around the world vary widely in the practice of OBED principles. Those that use OBED principles see growth and wealth accumulation; those that don't see struggle and poverty. While we can't say that OBED principles are the only cause of economic vitality, we can say that practicing them is positive for countries, economies, and people.

We can see that accelerators such as foreign direct investment, investment in human capital, sound economic policy, and diversification yield positive results. Political instability, corruption, and relying on foreign aid yield negative results. Each country must choose its path, hopefully moving on a positive trajectory of leaving no asset untapped and no transaction ignored.

10

A FLOURISHING ECONOMY: OBED AND THE WAY FORWARD

Haiti became the first black republic in the world in 1804 after a courageous and fierce fight against France, one of the world's superpowers at that time. This fight for freedom was the first time in history a black nation threw off its oppressor, and it led other nations to do the same. Brazil and most African nations, plus others around the world, now enjoy freedom thanks to Haiti's example. However, Haiti is no longer the leader it was more than two centuries ago. The small nation is trailing after most of the countries it showed how to become free.

Instead of taking the necessary steps to modernize its economy and create wealth, Haiti has a long and violent history filled with rebellions, coups, dictatorial leaders, corruption, natural disasters, and chaos. After gaining its independence, following decades of rebellions and international meddling, the nation seemed to fight against itself. Today the political climate is rocky and the economy a mess, with widespread unemployment and underemployment continuing to be a problem.

When political strife reigns, the economy suffers. When the economy suffers, the people suffer. When the people suffer, they leave. Or try to. In early January 2019, the U.S. Coast Guard intercepted a boat carrying seventy Haitian migrants headed to the United States. Upon discovery the boat turned around and, escorted by the USCG vessel, headed home.[370] Unfortunately this urge to leave is nothing new; Haitians have been leaving the country (or trying to) in high numbers since the 1970s.

These migrants are likely seeing the United States as a place of safety and jobs. They could find work, make more money than in Haiti, and begin to build enough wealth to send some home to relatives in need. Their homeland isn't providing enough opportunities to get education and high-paying jobs that allow them to live a better life. The country isn't providing a strong enough foundation for meaningful transactions and building wealth, so how can its citizens succeed?

That is the premise of this book: countries can improve their economies, improve the climate for business, and improve lives by following the few key principles of Opportunity-Based Economic Development. We've shown here that OBED principles work if countries apply them diligently. My homeland has failed to do this to its detriment; other countries around the globe have failed, or at least partially so, as well.

Greece has been rocked by financial drama created in part by disparity between spending and revenue. Yemen's brutal civil war has ruined its economy. Venezuela's leadership and policies have forced an economic catastrophe and millions have fled the country. North Korea's oppressive regime has decimated the nation. These countries have not been creating enough economic value; instead they have been losing value as they deal with war, political instability, corruption, and other issues. They are going in the opposite direction than most of the world today.

Numerous countries, on the other hand, have become highly successful as they work hard to create a vibrant economy that puts OBED principles into practice. One of these is Singapore.

SINGAPORE'S EXPLOSIVE GROWTH

Singapore is just 433 square miles of land area and has a 3 million-strong labor force, but its annual GDP of over $300 billion is higher than 75 percent of the world.[371] The Port of Singapore is the world's busiest transshipment port, and the world's second busiest behind Shanghai in terms of tonnage handled.[372]

How did this country that gained independence in 1965 (162 years after Haiti) go from a wasteland of unemployment, slums, and inadequate sanitation, water, and infrastructure to one of the top economies of the world?[373]

By applying all of the OBED principles we talk about in this book. Singapore didn't have this book as a guide, but the city-nation used all of our OBED principles in one way or another. It used accelerators to not only create transactions but to create superior transactions that put it at the top of the economic mountain.

OBED Principle 1 states that countries that create growth, wealth, and jobs do so as they increasingly move their share of job creation, GDP growth, and private investment from Agriculture to Industry to Services as the basis for the economy. When Singapore gained its independence, there was rampant unemployment. Most people worked in trade or services, when they worked at all, with almost no agricultural component to its economy.[374]

Leaders devised a plan to move forward with a program of industrialization (skipping Agriculture), focusing on labor-intensive industries that took advantage of the many unemployed workers in the nation (Principle 2). But with its history of enmity with its neighbors and limited trading possibilities close to home, Singapore opted first to look for trading partnerships with Europe and the United States.[375]

It began to create an environment that attracted investors. The government—its somewhat draconian measures can be debated—cracked down on corruption and the drug trade to ensure that investors could see a return from profitable businesses.[376] Singapore drafted business-friendly laws and created a stable business climate that began to appeal to international investors.[377] By 1972, just seven years after independence, a quarter of the country's manufacturing businesses were either foreign-owned or joint-venture companies. Japan and the United States were major investors.[378]

Singapore also began educating its population to work in IT, electronics, petrochemicals, tourism, and transportation to meet the needs of the many new employers (Principle 3). Technical schools were created, with Singapore also paying its investors to train workers in high-skilled industrial jobs.[379] As companies continued to do business in Singapore, the export picture changed. In the early years of independence, major exports were low-cost goods such as textiles, clothing, and basic electronics. Twenty years later, Singapore's workers were "engaging in wafer fabrication, logistics, biotech research, pharmaceuticals, integrated circuit design, and aerospace engineering."[380]

Today Singapore's economy continues to grow. Tourism is huge, attracting more than 10 million visitors each year to its casino resorts and through its medical and culinary tourism industries.[381] Banking has become a growth area, as has biotech and oil refining.[382] Over three thousand multinational corporations operate there, accounting for more than two-thirds of manufacturing and export sales.[383]

Singapore's use of accelerators is clear: pro-business and pro-investment policies; educating its workforce; attracting and keeping foreign direct investment; a stable economic environment; willingness to invest in new technologies; and growing its Services sector by investment in tourism and banking.

The country has also diversified within sectors as it sees opportunities. Oil refining, in the Industry sector, has been developed as an economic growth area and continues to be a vital part of the economy. Tourism has also been a key growth area within Services.[384] While Agriculture contributes very little to the economy, within that sector the country is focusing on agro-technology and creating agro-tech parks, in which modern farms use technology to produce more goods for use at home and to export to nearby countries (Principle 2).[385]

Singapore, a small island city-state, has become a giant in the economic world. Its GDP/PPP has grown from $66 billion in 1990 to $527 billion in 2017, an almost 700 percent increase in less than thirty years.[386] Crime rates are among the lowest in the world,[387] and universal health care is provided via a combination of government subsidies, insurance, and savings programs.[388] Singaporeans have benefited from the wealth of the country as a whole (Principle 4). It has tapped into its assets—human capital, intellectual capital, trading partnerships, and natural capital such as ports—to create superior transactions and vast wealth (Principle 5) for the country and its citizens.

CREATING WEALTH FASTER

As we have seen through the Agriculture-Industry-Services continuum, countries can no longer rely on traditional industries to create jobs and wealth. Consumer goods like textiles, garments, and other low-yield products don't bring enough wealth to allow businesses to expand, or low-skilled and uneducated workers to move beyond subsistence wages. Income inequality becomes an issue when too many low-paid workers keep wages low and profits for owners high. Yet there are many instances where Industry does create higher levels of wealth (creation of capital goods, technology, etc.), and countries can invest more heavily in these industries to create a stronger economy. Countries should invest in Industry if their assets can be used well there, and if accelerators can help create more superior transactions.

Yet to create wealth faster and exponentially, countries must look to enablers such as human capital, intellectual capital, computing, and data development. With these kinds of assets, the transformation from assets into marketable opportunities takes less time and requires fewer resources. Think about it: Is it cheaper to build a multi-acre complex on prime waterfront property to build ships, or an office building to house a bank of servers for an IT company? Which offers higher rewards based on market needs?

Is it better for a country to continue to focus on its low-yield garment industry or high-cost Industry base, or move toward becoming a hub for customer service call centers? Which workers are paid more? Which workers contribute more to the nation's economy? Which workers continue to grow in knowledge and tech experience?

Understanding and using assets such as human and intellectual capital can be a major breakthrough and offer real opportunities for struggling countries. As we've seen in the example of Nauru, mining has done much for the country; its real future, however, lies in developing other assets such as its human and intellectual capital. By this we mean using the brainpower of its people to create jobs in tech and service fields instead of using the backs of its people to mine phosphate, a mostly-depleted asset that has ruined a good portion of the island.

The world has changed dramatically in the last thirty years. A billion people have risen out of extreme poverty since 1990. Then there were 1.85 billion people living on less than $1.90 a day; as of 2015, that number had dropped to 736 million.[389] East and Central Asia and Europe have reduced extreme poverty to below 3 percent; more than half of the world's people in extreme poverty live in Sub-Saharan Africa.[390] The majority of the world's poor are young (under eighteen), live in rural areas, lack education, and are employed in the Agriculture sector.[391]

The world is wealthier today than it was at the turn of the millennium despite threats of climate change, war, terrorism, political extremism, mass migrations, immigration problems, and population growth. Medical breakthroughs and better medical care for the world's poor have increased life expectancy; women around the world have improved their lives, and that of their families, through economic empowerment; advancements in technology, research and development, and AI (artificial intelligence) have brought increased wealth to businesses, countries, and individuals. The world's population has increased, but extreme poverty has decreased.

Such progress has debunked old thinking such as the Malthusian Theory of Population. Thomas Malthus, an English cleric/scholar, published his theory in 1789 in "An Essay on the Principle of Population." Broadly, his theory states that population grows faster than food supply, which leads to a shortage of food, which leads to corrections in the form of man-made checks such as war, family planning, and celibacy, and natural checks such as floods and earthquakes.[392]

OBED theory, however, stipulates that as long as wealth generation is proportional to population growth, wealth creation and well-being of citizens should move upward equally as long as purchasing power is ensured via investments and transactions. Population growth versus purchasing power determines the level of opportunity for economic growth. If the number of people grows and so do their wages, the growth is viable when guaranteed by market dynamics through investments. Also, that growth isn't just a finite number, but rather includes the intelligence and resources needed to proactively generate and produce new wealth. It also includes a measure of the conducive environment needed for such transformations to happen. Wealth creation has no cap, no deadline, and no limits.

TRANSFORMING ASSETS INTO OPPORTUNITY

Countries such as Haiti are stuck because they can't transform human, intellectual, and natural assets into market opportunities. The opportunity to boost purchasing power through steady jobs requires tapping into additional and wealthier markets, but 80 percent of Haitians live on less than $2 a day. Such a low income level isn't enough to support the quantity or size of businesses needed to create the many jobs required for growth. There simply aren't enough people making enough money to allow enough businesses to succeed.

Having a higher number of businesses in Haiti that only focus on the local market—that create goods or services to sell to the 80 percent of the population living below the poverty line—would fail for lack of positive transactions. NGO purchasing power (NGOs buying goods in Haiti for dispersal in the country) and increasing exports would help Haiti, just as increasing exports helped China, India, and other countries. Their citizens are now enjoying a good enough income to sustain internal growth in those countries. Think of what business process outsourcing would do for Haiti. It could provide a marvelous economic push, with the right infrastructure and educational opportunities.

Haiti and other developing countries can be like a business that ignores consumer preferences. Eventually those businesses fail because consumers don't want or need the goods offered. Some countries, no matter what industries are developed and marketed to the world, still fail because they stick to the same old paths and practices. They stick with the least profitable and least-needed industries, failing or choosing to not understand how to turn the economy around through accelerators such as foreign direct investment, banking tools, value chain, asset management, and technology.

The Haitian economy, as well as the economies of other failing nations, is out of sync with economic reality. Leaders aren't even considering growth in competitive sectors that create jobs and see double-digit growth around the world. Leaders aren't putting policies in place that encourage more businesses to pursue opportunities, which would enlarge the economy and create more wealth. Haiti's biggest businesses are owned by about 1 percent of the population; the owners don't want more competition because their monopolies represent the status quo and are supported by politicians eager to please business interests.

As the manufacturing of capital goods, tech-related products, growing capital markets, and Service industries create massive wealth around the world, Haiti settles for consumer goods and low-margin products such as shirts. Clothing represents Haiti's largest sub-sector within Manufacturing, accounting for 90 percent of exports and about 10 percent of the country's gross domestic product.[393] Agriculture production (when it's not destroyed by natural disasters) yields little profit, especially when those agricultural products are exported in their natural states instead of taking advantage of the value chain like Ivory Coast does with its cocoa beans.

Despite being geographically close to the United States, the wealthiest nation in the world and a potential trading/export gold mine, Haiti is still poor. Singapore is geographically close to its biggest trading partner, China,[394] and is one of the top economies in the world. The two countries can't compare at even the most basic levels.

Haiti's economy is not performing at a level that will move its citizens out of poverty. The growth rate is simply insignificant. While the future for Haiti is bright when considering the opportunities, the challenges are equally significant. The country remains stagnant at this point. The only way forward is through better leadership and a drastic change of direction for the economy. The same can be said for other struggling countries around the world.

What can leaders do to encourage their countries to follow the OBED path? In a world where climate change, terrorism, wars, inflation, droughts, desertification, pollution, income inequality, inflation, and other powerful issues dominate, is it possible for a country to move forward economically by harnessing assets and creating superior transactions?

The simple answer is yes. Despite the global issues that abound, countries can begin to move forward by looking at their assets (and liabilities) and setting strategies that turn them into transactions. Iceland, for instance, has turned its volcanoes into geothermal energy. Icelanders use geothermal energy to heat water, create steam to drive turbines that create electricity, heat greenhouses to grow vegetables, warm up water so fish can breed, and even heat sea water and harvest the salt.[395]

BRICS countries—Brazil, Russia, India, China, South Africa— are emerging economies that have agreed to trade and investment cooperation between the five, as well as activities that benefit specific sectors.[396] BRICS countries accounted for 11 percent of the world's GDP in 1990, that number rising to almost 30 percent in 2014.[397] Each of the countries improved in significant ways during that time. China was below 3 percent of worldwide manufacturing output in 1990, and by 2015 that number had risen to about 25 percent. India focused on the Services sector, which is now at 61 percent of its GDP.[398]

Brazil's economic and social programs helped raise 29 million out of poverty between 2004 and 2014; Russia had 29 percent living below the poverty line in 2000, and 11 percent by 2012. South Africa's exports were at $27 million in 1990 and nearly five-fold higher by 2011.[399] While these countries still have far to go in some areas, they are moving forward in sector growth and in improving the lives of citizens.

Our proven OBED principles must be supported by the rule of law, sound policies, education, infrastructure, health care, and so on. When all that comes together, it triggers economic transformation. OBED principles are so powerful that even countries with a rough climate, like Iceland, can practice OBED and succeed. Other countries with "liabilities" can also find success when those liabilities are utilized wisely.

OBED principles highlight the need for countries to look for ways to use assets to create superior transactions. It may be easy to envision factories producing goods for export, but in the twenty-first century the real growth areas tap into the vast human resources available. Fields such as technology, banking and finance, AI, robotics, interactive learning, women entrepreneurship, analytical and data mining, alternative energies, digital footprint and security, and technologies we haven't dreamt of yet are where successful countries are heading as they use the brainpower of their human assets.

Manufacturing, mining, agriculture, and tourism are excellent sources of wealth and are good for countries to create and maintain if their assets dictate movement in those areas. But it's possible for countries to succeed without a substantial agriculture component (think Singapore and Iceland). Those countries understand that they need to leverage and succeed in other sectors to generate enough wealth to meet food needs through imports and still realize net positive transactions within their economies.

PATHS TO SUCCESS

Should developing countries adopt the strategy of skipping Agriculture altogether? The answer is no. They should leverage their most competitive sectors first, especially Agriculture and Manufacturing, then move forward on the OBED path toward Services. As countries move forward, the percentage of GDP and employment will begin to drop in Agriculture and Manufacturing. More workers will be employed in the higher-yield sectors even as Agriculture and Manufacturing output increases thanks to better technology in those areas.

Automation, in fact, is well on its way to reimagining the Manufacturing sector. Automation doesn't replace Manufacturing, but it does reexamine the number of workers needed in that sector. Manufacturing will still exist whether production is automated or not; it simply reduces the number of people employed in the sector and the percentage of GDP created by the sector.

Mechanization has already taken over most jobs in Agriculture (think tractors, bailers, and planters instead of people sowing seeds by hand and harvesting with a scythe), and is moving quickly into Manufacturing as robots and other machines do the jobs once done by humans. This isn't a bad thing at all; automation increases output in the sector, which benefits the economy as a whole. While it decreases the number of employees, the employees it does require are better educated in the high-end computers and robotics needed to keep the automated machines going. And better educated means better paid.

Developing countries, as should all countries, must prepare for increased automation by looking ahead to jobs that won't be as impacted by it or at new jobs that could be created by it through OBED. Countries must also look at where else to create jobs within the sector as well as outside it. Automation and mechanization aren't a death knell to the Manufacturing sector, just as it wasn't to the Agriculture sector.

Growing crops that help feed the population didn't stop; it's just that fewer people were needed to grow the same amount of or more food thanks to mechanization. Manufacturing won't end either— we all need clothes to wear, pans to cook with, cars to drive, cell phones to communicate with. It's just that fewer people are needed to produce the consumer and capital goods we use every day. Fewer resources are needed to create bigger output.

Investment, therefore, must move to more productive areas within sectors, to more productive sectors overall such as Services, and to sectors that might exist in the future. Artificial intelligence, automation, robot density (74 is the average number of robots used per 10,000 workers around the world[400]), and mechanization aren't going away and will only grow in importance. It isn't clear yet to what level AI and robotization will remove workers from all sectors; suffice it to say these things are and will continue to impact the global economy.

Leaders, therefore, must make decisions now that look to the future. Instead of focusing on growth in sectors with lower productivity and GDP share, leaders can encourage investment in sectors that promise growth. Leaders can pave the way for future wealth with policy decisions that encourage growth, with long-range infrastructure goals that facilitate connectivity, and with a focus on reducing corruption and political upheaval.

We want to show lawmakers and leaders that economic development is elastic and adaptable, that the real goal is wealth creation and the well-being of citizens. The reality is that countries are different, their comparative and competitive advantages are different, and each one's path is different. We don't expect countries with extreme land limitations to start their economic development journey in the Agriculture sector, nor do we expect countries with vast amounts of arable land to ignore it completely because evidence shows the sector creates little employment and contributes minimally to GDP growth today.

We don't want countries to avoid Manufacturing because it can create income inequality. We don't want countries with a low-educated workforce to avoid investment in the Services sector. While the OBED road is solid and proven, countries need to adapt their paths to their own reality as they look to the future with policies and investment plans that will yield increased wealth for their citizens and the country as a whole. There is no law that says you have to apply every OBED principle described here; but you should follow and apply the principles that work best in each country's situation. OBED is designed to liberate, not restrict.

No person and no country need to be poor anymore. Poverty, especially extreme poverty, is absolutely unnecessary. We have identified what creates both wealth and poverty and shared it in this book, so countries can begin to take steps to create one and avoid the other. Leadership with a wealth-creation mindset is the key. Any leader can choose to embrace poverty creation or embrace wealth creation. By electing or appointing leaders who embrace wealth creation, a country is well on its way to positive outcomes. Using the roadmap provided by OBED, we hope to see leaders leading their countries toward growth in the near future and the next decades.

TAKING THE NEXT STEPS

What does that leadership look like? It looks like lawmakers, business owners, youth associations, grassroots organizers, women's organizations, chambers of commerce, investors, and all other stakeholders playing their parts in the country's growth. Society isn't made up of only politicians and business owners; it's made up of citizens who can pressure them to make decisions that move a country forward. Citizens who can push for jobs, growth, and better lives.

We call on leaders to make policies that encourage investment locally and from abroad; to build or repair infrastructure; to root out corruption; to ease restrictions on new business creation; to think of the future in terms of technology and human capital. We call on all stakeholders to look to their futures and the future of their homelands, and participate in putting OBED principles in place. By doing so, their countries can succeed and citizens prosper.

OBED offers a proven path to self-sustainability. We encourage leaders to evaluate each step in light of economic goals that will lead to increased wealth and a better life for all citizens. Here are steps you can take to start on the OBED path. Carefully consider each one as you move forward.

1. Evaluate each sector to find the ones with the most growth potential (jobs and wealth). Each sector offers opportunities, but which ones offer the most and best opportunities?

2. Find out within those sectors the assets and liabilities that can be leveraged for growth. Does the Manufacturing sector offer room for value chain development? Could Services take advantage of an educated, multilingual workforce?

3. Rank those assets according to potential for wealth and job creation. Prioritizing assets helps leaders know where to focus efforts and investment.

4. Use economic formulas to determine rates of return on investment for those assets. Once assets are prioritized, using proven formulas to predict return on investment will help investors and business leaders determine where to focus efforts.

5. Develop a plan to attract local and international investors to pursue those opportunities. Plans can include posting research results, creating prospectus reports, inviting investors to visit, and forming consortiums to attract even more interest.

These are the basic steps to take, but there are other, deeper things to consider as you move forward with your OBED plans. These opportunity-supporting factors are just as important and should be carefully considered.

1. Take a hard look at the vision you have for your country, then calculate the steps it will take to get there. Where are you on the OBED scale? What do you have to do to put OBED principles into action? Identifying the necessary steps to achieve a wealthy and healthy economy takes detailed analysis, open and honest discussions among leaders, and a willingness to face hard truths and difficult issues.

2. Assess local support factors (country, region, city) by asking these questions:

   a. Does the healthcare system meet needs? What populations are underserved? Are medicines available? Is preventative medicine widely practiced?

   b. Is the educational system market oriented and training people to meet workforce demands?

   c. Does infrastructure—highways, bridges, ports, air travel, Internet and wireless services, and communications systems—work well and move information and goods in a timely manner?

   d. Does the banking system work well enough to foster FDI, local investment, currency controls, tough security measures, etc.?

3. Assess macro-indicators in these areas:

   a. Corruption. How much profit is siphoned by corrupt leaders or bureaucrats? Who is making the most money and why? How can corruption be halted?

   b. Human Development Index. What is the life expectancy of the population? How much education does a population have or can expect to have? What is the standard of living based on GDP per capita and other measures?

   c. Inflation. How high is inflation? Why is it high? If low, why?

   d. Employment. What is the unemployment rate? What sectors employ the most people? What sectors are open to growth in employment numbers?

   e. Confidence. How confident are citizens in the government and leaders to make changes? How willing is the population to make changes?

We are well aware that the path to self-sustainability can be fraught with fear, economic insecurity, and resistance. Yet we also offer a way forward that is guaranteed to bring growth and wealth to any country willing to take the necessary steps and put the necessary pieces in place. We've looked at countries who have used OBED principles in the past, and you may have looked at your country's past to assess what went wrong (or right).

Using the steps listed above and examples throughout this book, we encourage you to envision an economy that provides good jobs, that creates superior transactions, that grows personal and national wealth, that draws investment, that improves citizens' well-being, and that looks to the future for inspiration in growing fields such as AI and technology.

OBED is a way forward, a way to a better future. Countries can move forward when they are willing to create policies, invest resources, invite help, measure results, and live in a positive and forward-looking mindset. We invite and encourage you to move forward on this path. We invite you into a flourishing economy based on OBED.

NOTES

1   The World Factbook: Ethiopia. 27 March 2018. https://www.cia.gov/library/publications/the-world-factbook/geos/et.html

2   Jean-Louis, Daniel. *From Aid to Trade: How Aid Organizations, Businesses, and Governments Can Work Together: Lessons Learned from Haiti.* Port-au-Prince, Haiti: Fresh Strategy Press, 66

3   The World Factbook: Ethiopia. 27 March 2018. https://www.cia.gov/library/publications/the-world-factbook/geos/et.html

4   Ethiopia is turning its trash into electricity." Cambridge Industries. 27 March 18. https://www.facebook.com/NowThisFuture/videos/1995368517170985/

5   Jean-Louis, *From Aid to Trade, 81*

6   Jean-Louis, *From Aid to Trade*, 81

7   Jean-Louis, *From Aid to Trade*, 59

8   Jean-Louis, *From Aid to Trade*, page 83

9   "Ethiopia: Remarkable Progress Over More Than a Decade." IMF, 4 December 2018. 18 March 2019. https://www.imf.org/en/News/Articles/2018/12/04/na120418-ethiopia-remarkable-progress

10   "The World Bank in Ethiopia: Overview." 10 October 2018. 18 March 2019. http://www.worldbank.org/en/country/ethiopia/overview

11   Ibid

12   Ethiopia is turning its trash into electricity." Cambridge Industries. 27 March 18. https://www.facebook.com/NowThisFuture/videos/1995368517170985/

13   Baptiste, Nathalie. "Are Foreign NGOs Rebuilding Haiti Or Just Cashing In?" 10 July 2015. 4 May 2018. http://fpif.org/are-foreign-ngos-rebuilding-haiti-or-just-cashing-in/

14   "Haiti-Travel and Tourism." Export.gov. 4 July 2018. https://www.export.gov/article?id=Haiti-Travel-and-Tourism

15   Gregson, Jonathan. "Poorest Countries in the World." 13 Feb. 2017. 9 July 2018. https://www.gfmag.com/global-data/economic-data/the-poorest-countries-in-the-world?page=12

16   "The World Facebook: Congo, Republic of the." 6 April 2018. https://www.cia.gov/library/publications/resources/the-world-factbook/geos/cf.html

17   Lee, Kwang-rin, Jung Ha Lee, Young Ick Lew, Bae-ho Hahn, Ki-baik Lee. "Korea." 6 March 2015. 9 April 2018. https://www.britannica.com/place/Korea#ref35021

18   Kim, Kwan S. "The Korean Miracle (1962-1980) Revisited: Myths and Realities in Strategy and Development." November 1991. https://kellogg.nd.edu/sites/default/files/old_files/documents/166_0.pdf

19   "Economic and social developments." 10 April 2018. https://www.britannica.com/place/South-Korea/Economic-and-social-developments
20   Irwan, Alexander (2007) "Real wages and class struggle in South Korea," Journal of Contemporary Asia, 17:4, 385-408, 10 April 2018. https://www.tandfonline.com/doi/abs/10.1080/00472338780000281

21   Ouattara, Alassane D. "The Asian Crisis: Origins and Lessons," address, 4 May 1998. 10 April 2018. https://www.imf.org/en/News/Articles/2015/09/28/04/53/sp050498a

22   Kim, Kwan S. "The Korean Miracle (1962-1980) Revisited"

23   Ibid

24   Ibid

25   Ibid

26   Ibid

27   Shen, Lucinda. "If You Bought Google at Its IPO Price, Here's How Much Richer You'd Be." 18 Aug. 2017. 30 April 2018. http://fortune.com/2017/08/18/google-ipo-price-investment/

28   "Countries with Most FDI in 2018." 25 January 2018. 1 May 2018. https://www.gfmag.com/topics/macroeconomy-and-globalization/countries-most-fdi-inflows-2018

29   Van Vliet, V. (2010). *Porter's Value Chain Analysis.* Retrieved [5-1-18] from ToolsHero: https://www.toolshero.com/management/value-chain-analysis-porter/

30   "Number of recreational visitors to the Grand Canyon National Park in the United States from 2008 to 2018 (in millions." 7 May 2018. https://www.statista.com/statistics/253878/number-of-visitors-to-grand-canyon-national-park/)

31   "Botswana-Mining." 18 July 2017. 1 May 2018. https://www.export.gov/article?id=Botswana-Mining

32   Vanderveen, Steve. "A Little Heintz History." 31 June 2016. 19 April 2018. https://www.linkedin.com/pulse/little-holland-mi-business-history-heinz-steve-vanderveen

33   Ibid

34   Ibid

35   Emid, Al. "Costa Rica: The FDI Success Story." 6 Feb 2015. 25 April 2018. https://www.gfmag.com/magazine/february-2015/costa-rica-fdi-success-story

36   Ibid

37   Ibid

38   Ibid

39   Ibid

40   Stubing, Darren. "Qatar's Revolutionary Independence." 11 April 2018. 25 April 2018. https://www.gfmag.com/magazine/april-2018/qatars-revolutionary-independence.

41   Ibid

42   Ibid

43   "Qatar will have enough milk by Ramadan: Balada." Anadolu News Agency, 10 March 2018. 25 April 2018. https://www.aljazeera.com/news/2018/03/qatar-milk-ramadan-baladna-180310171634022.html

44   Ibid

45   Ibid

46   Al Sayegh, Hadeel. "Qatar dairy producer Baladna to IPO in first half, expand into new areas." Reuters. 13 January 2018. 25 April 2018. https://www.reuters.com/article/us-gulf-qatar-ipo/qatar-dairy-producer-baladna-to-ipo-in-first-half-expand-into-new-areas-idUSKBN-1F301I

47   Basu, Kaushik. "This is what you need to know about Bangladesh's remarkable economic rise." World Economic Forum. 24 Apr 2018. 7 May 2018. https://www.weforum.org/agenda/2018/04/why-is-bangladesh-booming?utm_source=Facebook%20Videos&utm_medium=Facebook%20Videos&utm_campaign=Facebook%20Video%20Blogs

48   Ibid

49   "Carnton: History." Battle of Franklin Trust. 29 Oct 2018. https://boft.org/carnton/

50   Urquhart, Michael. "The employment shift to services: where did it come from? 21 June 2018. https://stats.bls.gov/opub/mlr/1984/04/art2full.pdf, p. 14

51   https://data.worldbank.org/indicator/SL.AGR.EMPL.ZS International Labour Organization, ILOSTAT database. Data retrieved in November 2017. Accessed 6-21-18

52   https://data.worldbank.org/indicator/SL.SRV.EMPL.ZS, Data retrieved in November 2017. Accessed 21 June 2018

53   https://data.worldbank.org/indicator/SL.SRV.EMPL.ZS, Data retrieved in November 2017. Accessed 21 June 2018.

54   Mohamed, Adan. "Manufacturing the future of Kenya – Africa's Industrial Hub." 5 Dec 2017. 15 June 2018.   https://www.capitalfm.co.ke/business/2017/12/manufacturing-future-kenya-africas-industrial-hub/

55   Ibid

56   Ibid

57   Ibid

58   Ibid

59   Ibid
60   Ibid

61   Kenya Leather Development Council. 15 June 2018. http://leathercouncil.go.ke/advisory-role/

62   Ibid

63   Muchira, Njiraini. "Smuggling, hides exports hurting bid to grow leather trade." 2 Feb 2018. 15 June 2018. http://www.thee-astafrican.co.ke/business/Smuggling--hides-exports-hurting-bid-to-grow-leather-trade/2560-4292682-14chiw9z/index.html

64   McCaig, Brian and Nina Pavcnik. "Moving out of agriculture: structural change in Vietnam." 29 Oct 2013. https://www.dartmouth.edu/~npavcnik/docs/Vietnam_structural_change_October_2013.pdf, 3

65   Ibid

66   Dinh, Do Duc. "Manufacturing and Industry in Vietnam: Three Decades of Reform." June 2016. http://www.thebrenthurstfoundation.org/workspace/files/manufacturing-and-industry-in-vietnam.pdf, 6

67   Ibid

68   Ibid
69   Ibid, 8
70   Ibid
71   Ibid, 6
72   Ibid, 5
73   Ibid
74   Ibid, 7
75   Ibid, 6
76   Ibid
77   Ibid
78   Ibid, 7
79   Ibid
80   Ibid, 10
81   *DR-HT Quisqueya Growth and Poverty*, Report No. 67186-LAC. 25 April 2012. A document of the World Bank, v

82   Ibid

83   Ibid, viii

84   "Industry: Manufacturing." http://countrystudies.us/dominican-republic/47.htm. U.S. Library of Congress. 19-6-2018.

85   Ibid

86   Ibid

87   "The Growing Economy of the Dominican Republic." 19-6-2018.   https://www.liveandinvestoverseas.com/country-hub/dominican-republic/dominican-republic-economy/

88   "Dominican Republic Shares Strong Tourism Numbers and Plans for Continued Growth." Dominican Republic Ministry of Tourism. 16-4-2018. 19-62018. https://globenewswire.com/news-release/2018/04/16/1472369/0/en/Dominican-Republic-Shares-Strong-Tourism-Numbers-and-Plans-for-Continued-Growth.html

89   "The World Bank in Dominican Republic: Overview." 26-3-2018. 21-6-2018. http://www.worldbank.org/en/country/dominicanrepublic/overview#3

90   Ibid

91   "Free economic zones in the Dominican Republic." 3-2014. 30-3-2019. http://arichyhomes.com/free-economic-zones-in-the-dominican-republic/

92   Hyland, Pat. "The Dominican Republic: A Thriving Caribbean Destination." 13-3-2017. 23-6-2018. https://www.tourism-review.com/tourism-industry-in-the-dominican-republic-growing-news5322

93   Ibid

94   The World Factbook: Dominican Republic. 22-6-18. https://www.cia.gov/library/publications/the-world-factbook/geos/dr.html

95   Ibid

96   Burton, James. "25 Countries Who Don't Invest Much in Agriculture." World Atlas. 1 Dec. 2017. 26 June 2018. https://www.worldatlas.com/articles/the-countries-producing-the-least-agriculture-worldwide.html

97   Burton, James. "Countries With The Least Arable Land." World Atlas. 1-Dec. 17. 29-June-18. https://www.worldatlas.com/articles/the-least-agricultural-countries-in-the-world.html

98   "Haiti—Agriculture Sector." 26 June 2017. 26 June 2018. https://www.export.gov/article?id=Haiti-Agricultural-Sector

99   Viviano, Frank. "This Tiny Country Feeds the World." National Geographic, Sept. 2017. 7 July 2018. https://www.national-geographic.com/magazine/2017/09/holland-agriculture-sustainable-farming/

100   Ibid

101   Ibid

102   Ibid

103   Ibid

104   Ibid

105   Ibid

106   Ibid

107   Ibid

108   Ibid

109   Ibid

110   Ibid

111 "Europe's One-Stop Shop for Manufacturing Success." 13 July 2018. https://investinholland.com/business-operations/manufacturing/

112 Askew, Katy. "Kraft Heinz establishes Netherlands as 'global growth engine." 25 May 2018. 13 July 2018. https://www.foodnavigator.com/Article/2018/05/25/Kraft-Heinz-establishes-Netherlands-as-global-growth-engine

113 Ibid

114 "Kraft Heinz Opens Global Center of Excellence in Holland." 31 May 2018. 13 July 2018. https://investinholland.com/kraft-heinz-opens-global-center-of-excellence-in-holland/

115 "Wherever There's Water, There's Damen." 31 July 2018 https://www.damen.com/en/about/a-family-history

116 Ibid

117 Ibid

118 "Banking in the Netherlands: Statistics & Facts." 6 July 2018. https://www.statista.com/topics/3442/the-banking-sector-in-the-netherlands/

119 "Overview of Financial Stability." 6 July 2018. https://www.dnb.nl/en/binaries/423770_1600160_OFS_Spring_2016_WEB_tcm47-340663.PDF

120 Ibid

121 Ibid

122 "Europe's One-Stop Shop for Manufacturing Success." 6 July 2018. https://investinholland.com/business-operations/manufacturing/

123 "Overview of Financial Stability." 6 July 2018. https://www.dnb.nl/en/binaries/423770_1600160_OFS_Spring_2016_WEB_tcm47-340663.PDF

124 Ibid

125   Whitfield, Lindsay. "How Countries become rich and reduce poverty: A review of heterodox explanations of economic development." DIIS Working Paper 2011:13 https://www.diis.dk/files/media/publications/import/extra/wp2011-13-lkw-how-countries-become-rich-web_2.pdf

126   "Switzerland—Agriculture." 2 July 2018. https://www.nationsencyclopedia.com/economies/Europe/Switzerland-AGRICULTURE.html

127   "Iceland." 1 July 2018. 2 July 2018. https://www.climatechange-post.com/iceland/agriculture-and-horticulture/

128   Sanon, Evens and Flora Charner. "Haitian mango farmers get assistance, but will fruit exports help the country?" Associated Press. 10 Aug. 2010. 14 Apr. 2019. https://www.foxnews.com/world/haitian-mango-farmers-get-assistance-but-will-fruit-exports-help-the-country

129   Mulderif, Rudolf. "Overview Global Mango Market." 5 Jan. 2018. 2 July 2018. http://www.freshplaza.com/article/187370/OVERVIEW-GLOBAL-MANGO-MARKET

130   Ibid

131   Aboa, Ange. "Ivory Coast aims to grind 1 million tonnes of cocoa beans by 2011." 23 June 2018. 27 June 2018. https://af.reuters.com/article/investingNews/idAFKBN1JJ075-OZABS.

132   Ibid

133   "Africa: Cote D'Ivoire." The World FactBook. 20 June 2018. 28 June 2018. https://www.cia.gov/library/publications/the-world-factbook/geos/iv.html

134   Ibid

135   Ibid

136   Ibid

137   Ibid

138   Ouattara, Amadou. "A Story on Farming." 28 June 2018. https://www.cocoalife.org/in-the-cocoa-origins/cocoa-life-in-cote-divoire/a-story-on-farming-in-cote-divoire.

139   "Olam International Cocoa Processing Facility." 14 April 2019. https://www.foodprocessing-technology.com/projects/olaminterntaionalcoc/

140   Ibid

141   Ibid

142   Ibid

143   Ibid

144   Ford, Tamasin. "The chocolate shops championing Ivory Coast cocoa." 2 June 2016. 3-July 2018. https://www.bbc.com/news/business-36417934

145   Ibid

146   Ibid

147   "Number of mobile cellular subscriptions in Cote d'Ivoire from 2000 to 2017 (in millions)." 31 July 2018. https://www.statista.com/statistics/497179/number-of-mobile-cellular-subscriptions-in-cote-d-ivoire/

148   "Number of mobile cellular subscriptions per 100 inhabitants in Haiti from 2000 to 2017." 31 July 2018. https://www.statista.com/statistics/502111/mobile-cellular-subscriptions-per-100-inhabitants-in-haiti/

149   "Mobile Fact Sheet." 5 Feb. 2018. 13 July 2018. http://www.pewinternet.org/fact-sheet/mobile/

150   OECD (2018), Income inequality (indicator). doi: 10.1787/459aa7f1-en (accessed on August 7, 2018)

151   Denton, Will. "Gini Index." 14 Aug. 2018. https://www.investopedia.com/terms/g/gini-index.asp

152   "Income Inequality." OECD Data. 14 Aug. 2018. https://data.oecd.org/inequality/income-inequality.htm#indicator-chart

153   "Poverty rate." OECD Data. 14 Aug. 2018. https://data.oecd.org/inequality/poverty-rate.htm#indicator-chart

154   Birdsong, Nicholas. "The Consequences of Economic Inequality." 5 Feb. 2015. 18 Aug. 2018. https://sevenpillarsinstitute.org/consequences-economic-inequality/

155   Ibid

156   Sulla, Victor; Zikhali, Precious. 2018. *Overcoming Poverty and Inequality in South Africa : An Assessment of Drivers, Constraints and Opportunities (English)*. Washington, D.C. : World Bank Group. http://documents.worldbank.org/curated/en/530481521735906534/Overcoming-Poverty-and-Inequality-in-South-Africa-An-Assessment-of-Drivers-Constraints-and-Opportunities

157   Ibid

158   Beaubien, Jason. "The Country with the World's Worst Inequality Is ..." NPR, 2018. 18 Aug. 2018. https://www.npr.org/sections/goatsandsoda/2018/04/02/598864666/the-country-with-the-worlds-worst-inequality-is

159   Ibid

160   "South Africa's Manufacturing industry page." Updated 24 July 2018. 28 Aug. 2018. https://www.southafricanmi.com/south-africas-manufacturing-industry.html

161   "Economic growth better than what many expected." 6 March 3018. 28 Aug. 2018. http://www.statssa.gov.za/?p=10985

162   Creamer, Terence. "Extreme inequality in South Africa is constraining growth and investment." 10 Apr. 2010. 10 Sept. 2018. http://www.engineeringnews.co.za/article/extreme-inequality-is-constraining-south-african-investment-and-growth-2018-04-10

163   Evans, Sarah. "Cheap labour could cost bosses in the long term." 15 May 2015. 28 Aug. 2018. https://mg.co.za/article/2015-05-14-cheap-labour-could-cost-bosses-in-the-long-term

164   "Quarterly Labour Force Survey." 15 May 2018. 28 Aug. 2018. http://www.statssa.gov.za/?p=11139 1

165   "South Africa Average Monthly Gross Wage." 28 Aug. 2018. https://tradingeconomics.com/south-africa/wages

166   Smith, Michael Nassen. "How inequality is wrecking SA's economy, and what we can do about it." 16 Oct. 2017. 28 Aug. 2018. https://www.businesslive.co.za/bd/opinion/2017-10-16-alarming-statistics—how—sas-economy-suffers-from-inequality/

167   Ibid

168   Ibid

169   "World Inequality Report 2018." https://wir2018.wid.world/conclusion.html

170   Ibid, part 4

171   Ibid

172   Ibid, part 2

173   Ibid

174   "How does income inequality affect our lives?" 26 Jan. 2019. https://www.oecd-ilibrary.org/docserver/9789264246010-6-en.pdf?expires=1548544357&id=id&accname=guest&checksum=AE9FF0BACBDF8C0E59FBB8F20F34D9D

175   Ibid

176   "Health." The Inequality Trust. 10 Feb. 2019. https://www.equalitytrust.org.uk/health

177   Newkirk, Vann R. "The American Health-Care System Increases Income Inequality." 2018. 19 Aug. 2018.   https://www.theatlantic.com/politics/archive/2018/01/health-care-income-inequality-premiums-deductibles-costs/550997/

178   Ibid

179   Evans, Kevin. "Inequality in Haiti," editorial. 2018. 19 Aug. 2018. http://www.tribune242.com/news/2018/jul/17/inequality-haiti/

180   Karagiannaki, Dr. Eleni and Dr. Abigail McKnight et al. "The Relationship between Inequality and Poverty: mechanism and policy options." 2017. 20 Aug. 2018. http://www.lse.ac.uk/assets/rich-media/channels/publicLecturesAndEvents/slides/20170802_1830_theRelationshipBetweenInequalityAndPoverty_sl.pdf

181   Ibid

182   Ibid

183   Ibid

184   Hsu, Sara. "High Income Inequality Still Festering in China." 2016. 20 Aug. 2018. https://www.forbes.com/sites/sarahsu/2016/11/18/high-income-inequality-still-festering-in-china/#2281397d1e50

185   Ibid

186   Ibid

187 Ibid

188 The WID.World Project and the Measurement of Economic Inequality, Part V—Tackling Economic Inequality. 30 Aug. 2018. https://wir2018.wid.world/part-5.html

189 Ibid

190 Ibid

191 Drucker, Jesse and Simon Bowers. "After a Tax Crackdown, Apple Found a New Shelter for Its Profits." 6 Nov. 2017. 30 Aug. 2018. https://www.nytimes.com/2017/11/06/world/apple-taxes-jersey.html

192 Ibid

193 Ibid

194 The WID.World Project and the Measurement of Economic Inequality, Part V—Tackling Economic Inequality. 30 Aug. 2018. https://wir2018.wid.world/part-5.html

195 Ibid

196 "Education Inequality: How Income Inequality Blurs Education As The Great Equalizer." FinancesOnline. 30 Aug. 2018. https://financesonline.com/education-inequality-how-income-inequality-blurs-education-as-the-great-equalizer/

197 Lobosco, Kate. "Student loan debt just hit $1.5 trillion. Women hold most of it." 5 June 2018. 30 Aug. 2018. https://money.cnn.com/2018/06/05/pf/college/student-loan-stats/index.html

198 "Higher Education." 30 Aug. 2018. https://www.government.nl/topics/secondary-vocational-education-mbo-and-higher-education/higher-education

199 Ibid

200 "Haiti Economy Profile 2018." 31 Aug. 2018. https://www.indexmundi.com/haiti/economy_profile.html

201 Ibid

202 "Germany Economy-Overview." 31 Aug. 2018. https://www.indexmundi.com/germany/economy_overview.html

203 Kim, Kwan S. "The Korean Miracle (1962-1980) Revisited: Myths and Realities in Strategy Development." 1991. https://kellogg.nd.edu/sites/default/files/old_files/documents/166_0.pdf. 8-31-2018

204 2018 Index of Economic Freedom: South Korea. 31 Aug. 2018. https://www.heritage.org/index/country/southkorea

205 Salinas, Sara. "Amazon narrows the list of metro areas for its new headquarters to 20." 18-1-18. 10 Sept. 2018. https://www.cnbc.com/2018/01/18/amazon-narrows-list-of-candidates-for-new-headquarters-hq2-to-20.html

206 Ibid

207 Da Costa, Pedro Nicolaci. "A technology gap between the rich and poor is deepening US inequality." 4 May 2017. 10 Sept. 2018. https://www.businessinsider.com/technology-gap-deepening-us-inequality-2017-5

208 Ibid

209 Ibid

210 Qureshi, Zia. "Globalization, technology, and inequality: It's the policies, stupid." 16 Feb., 2018. 10 Sept. 2018. https://www.brookings.edu/blog/up-front/2018/02/16/globalization-technology-and-inequality-its-the-policies-stupid/

211   Russell-Prywata, Louise. "How Corruption Drives Inequality." 17 Jan. 2018. 10 Sept. 2018. https://inequality.org/research/corruption-drives-inequality/

212
Ibid

213   Jean-Louis, Daniel and Jacqueline Klamer. *From Aid to Trade*, 67. Fresh Strategy Press, 2016.

214   "About Adam Smith." Adam Smith Institute. 20 Sept. 2018. https://www.adamsmith.org/about-adam-smith/

215   Ibid

216   Ibid

217   Ibid

218   Ibid

219   Porter, Michael E. "The Five Competitive Forces That Shape Strategy." Harvard Business Review, Jan. 2008.10 Sept. 2018. https://hbr.org/2008/01/the-five-competitive-forces-that-shape-strategy

220   Ibid

221   Ibid

222   "How Foreign Direct Investment Can Contribute to Economic Development in Haiti." June 2018. https://www.youtube.com/watch?v=wYe7Eqivihg&t=6s

223   Ibid

224   Ibid

225   "David Ricardo: 1772–1823." The Library of Economics and Liberty. 8 Oct. 2018. https://www.econlib.org/library/Enc/bios/Ricardo.html

226 "Haiti—Market Opportunities." 26 June 2017. 18 Oct. 2018. https://www.export.gov/article?id=Haiti-Market-Opportunities.

227 Felicien, Marie Michelle. "New Harvesting Techniques Bring Hope to Haiti's Vetiver Farmers." 20 Sept. 2018. 18 Oct. 2018. https://globalpressjournal.com/americas/haiti/new-harvesting-techniques-bring-hope-haitis-vetiver-farmers/

228 Ibid

229 Ibid

230 Ibid

231 Ibid

232 Workman, Daniel. "Haiti's Top 10 Exports." World's Top Exports. 1 Apr. 2018. 25 oct. 2018. April 1, 2018. http://www.worldstopexports.com/haitis-top-10-exports/

233 Felicien, Marie Michelle. "New Harvesting Techniques Bring Hope to Haiti's Vetiver Farmers." 20 Sept. 2018. 18 Oct. 2018. https://globalpressjournal.com/americas/haiti/new-harvesting-techniques-bring-hope-haitis-vetiver-farmers/

234 Ibid

235 Ibid

236 Ibid

237 Ibid

238 Thompson, Karl. "The Rise and Fall of Detroit. 20 Sept. 2017. 24 Oct. 2018. https://revisesociology.com/2017/09/20/rise-fall-detroit-industrialisation/

239 Ibid

240   "The World Bank in Haiti." 21 Sept. 2018. 20 Nov. 2018. https://www.worldbank.org/en/country/haiti/overview

241   "The World Bank in Somalia." 12 Nov. 2018. 20 Nov. 2018. https://www.worldbank.org/en/country/somalia/overview

242   "The Population of Poverty USA." 20 Nov. 2018. https://povertyusa.org/facts

243   "Poverty Overview." 24 Sept. 2018. 20 Nov. 2018. https://www.worldbank.org/en/topic/poverty/overview

244   Bruenig, Matt. "Two Theories of Poverty." Blog. 28 May 2014. https://www.demos.org/blog/7/28/14/two-theories-poverty.

245   "Haiti GDP Annual Growth Rate." Nov. 2018. 24 Nov. 2018. https://tradingeconomics.com/haiti/gdp-growth-annual

246   Ibid

247   Ibid

248   Ibid

249   "Over 40% of the world's poorest will live in Nigeria, Congo by 2050." 19 Sept. 2018. 13 Feb. 2019.   https://www.vanguardngr.com/2018/09/over-40-of-worlds-poorest-will-live-in-nigeria-congo-by-2050-report/

250   "Haiti GDP." 13 Feb. 2019. https://tradingeconomics.com/haiti/gdp

251   "Doing Business 2019: A Year of Record Reforms, Rising Influence." The World Bank Group. 31 Oct. 2018. 15 Apr. 2019. https://www.worldbank.org/en/news/immersive-story/2018/10/31/doing-business-2019-a-year-of-record-reforms-rising-influence

252 Ibid

253 Ibid

254 Ibid

255 Ibid

256 "Country Profile: Rwanda." 15 Apr. 2019. http://databank. worldbank.org/data/views/reports/reportwidget.aspx?Report_Name=Coun tryProfile&Id=b450fd57&tbar=y&dd=y&inf=n&zm=n&country=RWA.

257 Ibid

258 Ibid

259 "The World Factbook: Syria." 15 Apr. 2019. https://www. cia.gov/library/publications/the-world-factbook/geos/sy.html

260 Ibid

261 Ibid

262 Ibid

263 "Syria: Economic Forecasts." Trading Economics. 31 Oct. 2018. https://tradingeconomics.com/syria/forecast

264 Ibid

265 "Nauru." 27 Nov. 2018. http://www.naurugov.nr/about-nauru/our-country.aspx

266 Obiols, Maria. "Countries with Highest GDP Growth in 2017." 18 Oct. 2017. 27 Nov. 2018. https://www.gfmag.com/global-data/economic-data/countries-highest-gdp-growth

267   "Nauru." The World Factbook. 19 Nov. 2018. 28 Nov. 2019.
https://www.cia.gov/library/publications/the-world-factbook/geos/
nr.html

268   "Find Industry and Manfacturing expertise in Nauru." 28
Nov. 2019. http://www.commonwealthofnations.org/sectors-nauru/
business/industry_and_manufacturing/

269   Pariona, Amber. "How Has Phosphate Mining In Nauru
Led to An Environmental Catastrophe?" 3 Nov. 2017. 6 Dec. 2018.
https://www.worldatlas.com/articles/how-phosphate-mining-in-
nauru-has-led-to-an-environmental-catastrophe.html

270   Ibid

271   "The World Factbook: Nauru." 19 Nov. 2018. 28 Nov. 2018.
https://www.cia.gov/library/publications/the-world-factbook/geos/
nr.html.

272   Ibid

273   Ibid

274   Ibid

275   "The World Bank in Finland." 7 Dec. 2018 http://www.world-
bank.org/en/country/finland/overview

276   "The World Bank: Finland." 15 Apr. 2019. https://data.
worldbank.org/country/finland

277   Ibid

278   "Finland." World Economic Forum. 11 Dec. 2018. http://
reports.weforum.org/pdf/gci4-2018/WEF_GCI4_2018_Profile_FIN.
pdf

279   Ibid

280   "Best Countries for Business." Forbes. 11 Dec. 2018. https://www.forbes.com/best-countries-for-business/list/#tab:overall

281   "Finland." Forbes. Dec. 2017. 11 Dec. 2018. https://www.forbes.com/places/finland/

282   Ibid

283   "Distribution of employment by economic sector in Finland from 2007-2017." Statista. 11 Dec. 2018. https://www.statista.com/statistics/328329/employment-by-economic-sector-in-finland/

284   "Finland GDP From Manufacturing." Trading Economics. 12 Dec. 2018. https://tradingeconomics.com/finland/gdp-from-manufacturing.

285   "Service Sector Provides 72.9% of all Jobs in Finland." Business Finland. 9 May 2012. 12 Dec. 2018. https://www.investin-finland.fi/-/service-sector-provides-72-9-of-all-jobs-in-finland

286   Hjerppe, Riitta. "An Economic History of Finland." 16 Dec. 2018. https://eh.net/encyclopedia/an-economic-history-of-finland/

287   Ibid

288   "Economy and Business Opportunities from Finland." GlobalTenders.com. 16 Dec. 2018. https://www.globaltenders.com/economy-of-finland.php/

289   "The World Bank in Botswana." Overview. 1 Nov. 2018 update. 19 Dec. 2018. http://www.worldbank.org/en/country/botswana/overview

290   Ibid

291   Ibid

292   Ibid

293   Smolnikova, Anastasia. "Diamond industry of Botswana, its current state and prospects." 15 Oct. 2018. 19 Dec. 2018. https://www.rough-polished.com/en/analytics/111968.html

294   Ibid

295   Shantyaei, Sanam. "Diamonds aren't forever: Botswana seeks to diversify its economy." 16 Dec. 2017. 18 Dec. 2018. https://www.france24.com/en/20171216-botswana-diamonds-industry-economy-sustainable-tourism-wildlife-safaris

296   Ibid

297   Ibid

298   Ibid

299   "Kazungula Bridge set to open corridor between Zambia, Botswana." African News Agency. 14 March, 2018. 19 Dec. 2018. http://www.engineeringnews.co.za/article/kazungula-bridge-set-to-open-corridor-between-zambia-botswana-2018-03-14

300   Ibid

301   Beaubien, Jason. "Botswana's 'Stunning Achievement' Against AIDS." 9 Apr. 2012, aired on Morning Edition. 21 Dec. 2018.   https://www.npr.org/2012/07/09/156375781/botswanas-stunning-achievement-against-aids.
302
Ibid

303   Ibid

304   "The World Factbook: Botswana." 8 Dec. 2018, update. 21 Dec. 2018. https://www.cia.gov/library/publications/resources/the-world-factbook/geos/bc.html

305   "Ghana." The World Bank. 30 Dec. 2018. https://data.world-bank.org/country/ghana

306 "Niche: Taste of Ghana." 30 Dec. 2018. http://nichecocoa. com

307 Ibid

308 Ibid

309 Ibid

310 McDonnell, Tim. "What's the World's Fastest Growing Economy? Ghana Contends for the Crown." 10 Mar. 2018. 30 Dec. 2018. https://www.nytimes.com/2018/03/10/world/africa/ghana-worlds-fastest-growing-economy.html

311 Crabtree, Justina. "Ghana is 'about to have an oil boom.'" 16 Mar. 2018. 30 Dec. 2018. https://www.cnbc.com/2018/03/16/ghana-is-about-to-have-an-oil-boom.html

312 Ibid

313 "Ghana-Oil and Gas." export.gov. 3 Dec. 2018. 30 Dec. 2018. https://www.export.gov/article?id=Ghana-Oil-and-Gas

314 Ibid

315 The World Bank. Data retrieved 9-2018. 30 Dec. 2018. https://data.worldbank.org/indicator/SL.SRV.EMPL.ZS?locations=GH

316 McDonnell, Tim. "What's the World's Fastest Growing Economy? Ghana Contends for the Crown." 10 Mar. 2018. 30 Dec. 2018. https://www.nytimes.com/2018/03/10/world/africa/ghana-worlds-fastest-growing-economy.html

317 "The World Factbook: Malaysia." 18 Dec. 2018. 31 Dec. 2018. https://www.cia.gov/library/publications/the-world-factbook/geos/my.html

318 Ibid

319　Ibid

320　"Malaysia's economic outlook very encouraging claims finance minister." 31 Dec. 2018. 31 Dec. 2018. https://www.channelnewsasia.com/news/asia/malaysia-economic-outlook-encouraging-lim-guan-eng-11075446

321　Ibid

322　"Malaysia: Economy." The Commonwealth. 31 Dec. 2018. http://thecommonwealth.org/our-member-countries/malaysia/economy
323　Ibid

324　Zainul, Emir. "Services sector to grow 5.9% y-o-y in 2019, says MoF." 2 Nov. 2018. 31 Dec. 2018. http://www.theedgemarkets.com/article/services-sector-grow-59-yoy-2019-says-mof

325　Ibid
326　"Malaysia's widening income gap between rich and poor." 16 Oct. 2018. 31 Dec. 2018. https://www.thestar.com.my/business/business-news/2018/10/16/malaysias-widening-income-gap/

327　Ibid

328　"The World Factbook: South Sudan." 16 Nov. 2018, update. 28 Nov. 2019. https://www.cia.gov/library/publications/the-world-factbook/geos/od.html

329　Ibid

330　Ibid

331　Ibid

332　Ibid

333　Ibid

334 "Best Countries for Business." Forbes. Dec. 2018. 15 Apr. 2019. https://www.forbes.com/places/greece/

335 "GINI index (World Bank estimate). 15-Apr. 2019. https://data.worldbank.org/indicator/SI.POV.GINI?locations=GR

336 "Best Countries for Business." Forbes. Dec. 2018. 15 Apr. 2019. https://www.forbes.com/places/greece/

337 Ibid

338 Johnston, Matthew. "Understanding the Downfall of Greece's Economy." Investopedia. 25 Oct. 2018. 3 Jan. 2019. https://www.investopedia.com/articles/investing/070115/understanding-downfall-greeces-economy.asp

339 Ibid

340 Ibid

341 Ibid

342 Ibid

343 Ibid

344 "The World Factbook: Libya." 21 Dec. 2018. https://www.cia.gov/library/publications/resources/the-world-factbook/geos/ly.html

345 Ibid

346 Ibid

347 Ibid

348 Ibid

349 Ibid

350 Ibid

351 Fasanotti, Federica Saini. "Making Libya's economy work again." 10-7-2016. 21 Dec. 2018. https://www.brookings.edu/blog/order-from-chaos/2016/10/07/making-libyas-economy-work-again/

352 "The World Factbook: Venezuela." 12 Dec. 2018, update. 31 DEC. 2018. https://www.cia.gov/library/publications/the-world-factbook/geos/ve.html

353 Ibid

354 Ibid

355 Ibid

356 Ibid

357 Heaphy, Edmund. "The pictures show how much cash Venezuelans needed to buy even basic goods." 21 Aug. 2018, in collaboration with Quartz. 31 Dec. 2018. https://www.weforum.org/agenda/2018/08/the-stacks-of-cash-needed-to-buy-basic-goods-tell-venezuela-s-insane-inflation-story

358 Pons, Corina and Tibisay Romero. "Venezuela cuts five zeros from currency as economic plan sows confusion." 20 Aug. 2018. 31 Dec. 2018. https://www.reuters.com/article/us-venezuela-economy/venezuela-cuts-five-zeros-from-currency-as-economic-plan-sows-confusion-idUSKCN1L51H7

359 Ibid

360 Nebehay, Stephanie. "Two million more Venezuelans could flee next year: U.N." 14 Dec. 2018. 31 Dec. 2018. https://www.reuters.com/article/us-venezuela-migration/two-million-more-venezuelans-could-flee-next-year-u-n-idUSKBN1OD2CD

361 Ibid

362 "The World Factbook: Yemen." 2 Jan. 2019. https://www. cia.gov/library/publications/the-world-factbook/geos/ym.html

363 Ibid

364 Ibid

365 Ibid

366 Ibid

367 Ibid

368 Ibid

369 Batha, Emma. "Yemen's plunging economy threatens to kill more people than war: aid agency." 4 Sept. 2018. 2 Jan. 2018. https://www.reuters.com/article/us-yemen-war-economy-hunger/ yemens-plunging-economy-threatens-to-kill-more-people-than-war- aid-agency-idUSKCN1LK1YL

370 Madan, Monique O. "A boat with 70 Haitians on way to U.S. turns around after confronted by Coast Guard." *The Miami Herald*, 6 Jan. 2019. 10 Jan. 2019. https://www.miamiherald.com/news/ local/immigration/article224000780.html

371 Zhou, Ping. "Singapore's Economic Development: Singapore Has Exemplified Dramatic Economic Growth in Asia." 16 Apr. 2018. 2 Jan. 2019. https://www.thoughtco.com/ singapores-economic-development-1434565

372 Ibid

373 Ibid

374 Ibid

375 Ibid

376   Ibid

377   Ibid

378   Ibid

379   Ibid

380   Ibid

381   Ibid

382   Ibid

383   Ibid

384   Ibid

385   "Singapore: Agricultural Sectors." 18 July 2018. 4 Jan.
2019. https://www.export.gov/article?id=Singapore-Agricultural-Sectors

386   "GDP, PPP. The World Bank." 12 Jan. 2019.
https://data.worldbank.org/indicator/NY.GDP.MKTP.
PP.CD?locations=SG
387   Saiidi, Uptin. "Singapore's crime rate is so low that many
shops don't even lock up." 16 Jan. 2018. 12 Jan. 2019. https://www.
cnbc.com/2018/01/16/singapores-crime-rate-is-so-low-that-many-shops-
dont-even-lock-up.html

388   Liu, Chang and William Haseltine. "The Singaporean
Health Care System." 12 Jan. 2019. https://international.common-
wealthfund.org/countries/singapore/

389   "Poverty Overview." The World Bank. 24 Sept. 2018. 11
Jan. 2019. https://www.worldbank.org/en/topic/poverty/overview

390   Ibid

391   Ibid

392   Agarwal, Preteek. "Malthusian Theory of Population." 2 Apr. 2018 update. 11 Jan. 2019. https://www.intelligenteconomist.com/malthusian-theory/

393   Schipani, Andrew. "Haiti's economy held together by polo shirts and blue jeans." *Financial Times*. 16 Apr. 2015. 16 Jan. 2019. https://www.ft.com/content/d39377d8-dd2f-11e4-975c-00144feab7de

394   Workman, Daniel. "Singapore's Top Trading Partners." 29 Aug. 2018. 12 Jan. 2019. http://www.worldstopexports.com/singapores-top-import-partners/

395   Tournadre, Morgan. "How to Use a Volcano: Iceland Edition." 2 Mar. 2016. 13 Jan. 2019. http://www.volcanohouse.is/2016/03/02/use-volcano-iceland-edition/

396   Majaski, Christina (rev). "Brazil, Russia, India and China—BRIC Definition." 25 Feb. 2019 update. 16 April. 2019. https://www.investopedia.com/terms/b/bric.asp

397   Bremmer, Ian. "The Mixed Fortunes of the BRICS Countries, in 5 Facts." 1 Sept. 2017. 14 Jan. 2019. http://time.com/4923837/brics-summit-xiamen-mixed-fortunes/

398   Ibid

399   Ibid

400   "Robot density rises globally." 7 Feb. 2018. 14 Feb. 2019. https://ifr.org/ifr-press-releases/news/robot-density-rises-globally

APPENDIX

Table 1
Country: Argentina
Growth in GDP Per Capita in the period 1995 – 2007: 28.84%

Sector	Asset	Amount	Relative Rank[2]	Sector Share 95[3]	Sector Share 07
Agriculture	KM2 arable land PC	0.008	2	5.79	8.78
Forestry	KM2 forest land PC	0.010	12	0.10	0.09
Industry	% of Population Unschooled	4.0	31	28.44	32.49
Services	Mean Years of Education	8.64	12	65.77	58.91
Tourism	Cultural & Natural Beauty[1]	4.08	13	0.99	1.70

1. Amount: Refers to score on a scale for Tourism Sector
2. Relative Rank: Strength of asset compared to other countries
3. Sector Share: Share of value added of total GDP that was added by sector

Table 2
Country: Bangladesh
Growth in GDP Per Capita in the period 1995 – 2007: 49.65%

Sector	Asset	Amount	Relative Rank[2]	Sector Share 95[3]	Sector Share 07

Agricul-ture	KM2 arable land PC	0.001	35	26.38	18.71
Forestry	KM2 forest land PC	0.000	38	15.33	16.74
Industry	% of Population Unschooled	50.8	3	24.56	25.74
Services	Mean Years of Education	3.68	37	49.06	55.56
Tourism	Cultural & Natural Beauty[1]	2.3	35	0.06	0.10

1. Amount: Refers to score on a scale for Tourism Sector
2. Relative Rank: Strength of asset compared to other countries
3. Sector Share: Share of value added of total GDP that was added by sector

Table 3
Country: Bolivia
Growth in GDP Per Capita in the period 1995 – 2007: 21.10%

Sector	Asset	Amount	Rela-tive Rank[2]	Sector Share 95[3]	Sector Share 07
Agricul-ture	KM2 arable land PC	0.003	16	16.88	12.88
Forestry	KM2 forest land PC	0.081	2	0.94	0.60
Industry	% of Population Unschooled	14.2	15	33.11	36.39
Services	Mean Years of Education	7.83	18	50.00	50.73
Tourism	Cultural & Natural Beauty[1]	3.55	17	1.68	2.75

1. Amount: Refers to score on a scale for Tourism Sector
2. Relative Rank: Strength of asset compared to other countries
3. Sector Share: Share of value added of total GDP that was added by sector

Table 4
Country: Botswana
Growth in GDP Per Capita in the period 1995 – 2007: 47.42%

Sector	Asset	Amount	Rela-tive Rank[2]	Sector Share 95[3]	Sector Share 07
Agricul-ture	KM2 arable land PC	0.002	24	4.91	2.49
Forestry	KM2 forest land PC	0.083	1	0.55	0.35
Industry	% of Population Unschooled	20.0	12	46.47	46.54
Services	Mean Years of Education	8.24	16	48.62	50.96
Tourism	Cultural & Natural Beauty[1]	3.59	16	3.70	4.97

1. Amount: Refers to score on a scale for Tourism Sector
2. Relative Rank: Strength of asset compared to other countries
3. Sector Share: Share of value added of total GDP that was added by sector

Table 5
Country: Brazil
Growth in GDP Per Capita in the period 1995 – 2007: 19.10%

Sector	Asset	Amount	Rela-tive Rank[2]	Sector Share 95[3]	Sector Share 07

Agricul-ture	KM2 arable land PC	0.004	13	5.77	5.18
Forestry	KM2 forest land PC	0.033	4	0.58	0.45
Industry	% of Population Unschooled	19.5	13	27.53	27.12
Services	Mean Years of Education	5.58	28	66.70	67.70
Tourism	Cultural & Natural Beauty[1]	6.01	1	0.15	0.38

1. Amount: Refers to score on a scale for Tourism Sector
2. Relative Rank: Strength of asset compared to other countries
3. Sector Share: Share of value added of total GDP that was added by sector

Table 6
Country: Chile
Growth in GDP Per Capita in the period 1995 – 2007: 42.58%

Sector	Asset	Amount	Rela-tive	Sector Share 95[3]	Sector Share 07
Agricul-ture	KM2 arable land PC	0.001	29	9.24	3.69
Forestry	KM2 forest land PC	0.011	9	0.78	0.52
Industry	% of Population Unschooled	4.5	29	42.34	43.35
Services	Mean Years of Education	8.78	11	55.47	52.61
Tourism	Cultural & Natural Beauty[1]	2.93	24	1.80	1.27

1. Amount: Refers to score on a scale for Tourism Sector
2. Relative Rank: Strength of asset compared to other countries
3. Sector Share: Share of value added of total GDP that was added by sector

Table 7
Country: China
Growth in GDP Per Capita in the period 1995 – 2007:
184.13%

Sector	Asset	Amount	Relative Rank[2]	Sector Share 95[3]	Sector Share 07
Agriculture	KM2 arable land PC	0.001	31	19.60	10.28
Forestry	KM2 forest land PC	0.001	31	0.77	0.18
Industry	% of Population Unschooled	16.0	14	46.75	46.86
Services	Mean Years of Education	6.79	25	33.65	42.86
Tourism	Cultural & Natural Beauty[1]	5.05	4	1.09	1.06

1. Amount: Refers to score on a scale for Tourism Sector
2. Relative Rank: Strength of asset compared to other countries
3. Sector Share: Share of value added of total GDP that was added by sector

Table 8
Country: Costa Rica
Growth in GDP Per Capita in the period 1995 – 2007: 38.75%

Sector	Asset	Amount	Rela-tive Rank[2]	Sector Share 95[3]	Sector Share 07
Agricul-ture	KM2 arable land PC	0.001	36	14.02	8.87
Forestry	KM2 forest land PC	0.007	15	2.90	1.38
Industry	% of Population Unschooled	6.3	24	29.17	26.76
Services	Mean Years of Education	7.42	22	56.82	64.37
Tourism	Cultural & Natural Beauty[1]	5.09	3	7.92	8.24

1. Amount: Refers to score on a scale for Tourism Sector
2. Relative Rank: Strength of asset compared to other countries
3. Sector Share: Share of value added of total GDP that was added by sector

Table 9
Country: Croatia
Growth in GDP Per Capita in the period 1995 – 2007: 70.81%

Sector	Asset	Amount	Rela-tive Rank[2]	Sector Share 95[3]	Sector Share 07
Agricul-ture	KM2 arable land PC	0.002	22	7.18	4.83
Forestry	KM2 forest land PC	0.004	18	0.23	0.20

Industry	% of Population Unschooled	6.5	23	32.31	28.10
Services	Mean Years of Education	9.08	8	60.51	67.07
Tourism	Cultural & Natural Beauty[1]	3.8	15	5.34	15.94

1. Amount: Refers to score on a scale for Tourism Sector
2. Relative Rank: Strength of asset compared to other countries
3. Sector Share: Share of value added of total GDP that was added by sector

Table 10
Country: Czech Republic
Growth in GDP Per Capita in the period 1995 – 2007: 49.77%

Sector	Asset	Amount	Relative Rank2	Sector Share 95[3]	Sector Share 07
Agriculture	KM2 arable land PC	0.003	18	4.37	2.17
Forestry	KM2 forest land PC	0.003	23	0.38	0.20
Industry	% of Population Unschooled	0.9	36	38.96	38.24
Services	Mean Years of Education	11.99	1	56.67	59.59
Tourism	Cultural & Natural Beauty[1]	2.59	29	4.86	4.40

1. Amount: Refers to score on a scale for Tourism Sector
2. Relative Rank: Strength of asset compared to other countries
3. Sector Share: Share of value added of total GDP that was added by sector

Table 11
Country: Dominican Republic
Growth in GDP Per Capita in the period 1995 – 2007: 65.87%

Sector	Asset	Amount	Rela-tive Rank[2]	Sector Share 95[3]	Sector Share 07
Agricul-ture	KM2 arable land PC	0.001	30	10.01	7.08
Forestry	KM2 forest land PC	0.002	29	0.05	0.03
Industry	% of Population Unschooled	4.8	28	33.80	31.04
Services	Mean Years of Education	6.31	26	56.20	61.88
Tourism	Cultural & Natural Beauty[1]	2.59	30	15.09	11.47

1. Amount: Refers to score on a scale for Tourism Sector
2. Relative Rank: Strength of asset compared to other countries
3. Sector Share: Share of value added of total GDP that was added by sector

Table 12
Country: Estonia
Growth in GDP Per Capita in the period 1995 – 2007: 141.01%

Sector	Asset	Amount	Rela-tive Rank[2]	Sector Share 95[3]	Sector Share 07
Agricul-ture	KM2 arable land PC	0.006	3	5.73	3.46

Forestry	KM2 forest land PC	0.015	7	1.68	0.46
Industry	% of Population Unschooled	0.9	37	31.89	30.83
Services	Mean Years of Education	10.38	4	62.37	65.72
Tourism	Cultural & Natural Beauty[1]	2.69	28	13.86	6.22

1. Amount: Refers to score on a scale for Tourism Sector
2. Relative Rank: Strength of asset compared to other countries
3. Sector Share: Share of value added of total GDP that was added by sector

Table 13
Country: Hungary
Growth in GDP Per Capita in the period 1995 – 2007: 53.13%

Sector	Asset	Amount	Relative Rank[2]	Sector Share 95[3]	Sector Share 07
Agriculture	KM2 arable land PC	0.005	6	8.39	3.98
Forestry	KM2 forest land PC	0.002	27	0.17	0.10
Industry	% of Population Unschooled	1.0	35	30.45	31.11
Services	Mean Years of Education	10.41	3	61.16	64.92
Tourism	Cultural & Natural Beauty[1]	2.72	26	6.61	4.13

1. Amount: Refers to score on a scale for Tourism Sector
2. Relative Rank: Strength of asset compared to other countries
3. Sector Share: Share of value added of total GDP that was

added by sector

Table 14
Country: India
Growth in GDP Per Capita in the period 1995 – 2007: 79.70%

Sector	Asset	Amount	Rela-tive Rank[2]	Sector Share 95[3]	Sector Share 07
Agriculture	KM2 arable land PC	0.002	27	26.26	18.93
Forestry	KM2 forest land PC	0.001	35	0.48	0.31
Industry	% of Population Unschooled	47.8	4	32.72	34.66
Services	Mean Years of Education	4.12	35	46.34	46.40
Tourism	Cultural & Natural Beauty[1]	4.42	8	0.72	0.98

1. Amount: Refers to score on a scale for Tourism Sector
2. Relative Rank: Strength of asset compared to other countries
3. Sector Share: Share of value added of total GDP that was added by sector

Table 15
Country: Indonesia
Growth in GDP Per Capita in the period 1995 – 2007: 24.28%

Sector	Asset	Amount	Rela-tive Rank[2]	Sector Share 95[3]	Sector Share 07
Agriculture	KM2 arable land PC	0.001	32	17.14	13.72

Forestry	KM2 forest land PC	0.006	16	1.15	0.63
Industry	% of Population Unschooled	32.5	6	41.80	46.80
Services	Mean Years of Education	4.62	34	41.06	39.48
Tourism	Cultural & Natural Beauty[1]	4.36	9	2.60	1.40

1. Amount: Refers to score on a scale for Tourism Sector
2. Relative Rank: Strength of asset compared to other countries
3. Sector Share: Share of value added of total GDP that was added by sector

Table 16
Country: Jordan
Growth in GDP Per Capita in the period 1995 – 2007: 39.87%

Sector	Asset	Amount	Rela-tive Rank[2]	Sector Share 95[3]	Sector Share 07
Agricul-ture	KM2 arable land PC	0.001	37	4.32	2.84
Forestry	KM2 forest land PC	0.000	37	0.03	0.02
Industry	% of Population Unschooled	24.0	9	28.92	31.62
Services	Mean Years of Education	7.58	19	66.75	65.54
Tourism	Cultural & Natural Beauty[1]	2.05	36	14.47	15.91

1. Amount: Refers to score on a scale for Tourism Sector
2. Relative Rank: Strength of asset compared to other countries
3. Sector Share: Share of value added of total GDP that was

added by sector

Table 17
Country: Kenya
Growth in GDP Per Capita in the period 1995 – 2007: 11.18%

Sector	Asset	Amount	Rela-tive Rank[2]	Sector Share 95[3]	Sector Share 07
Agricul-ture	KM2 arable land PC	0.002	25	31.13	23.27
Forestry	KM2 forest land PC	0.002	30	7.28	3.57
Industry	% of Population Unschooled	26.1	8	16.02	21.82
Services	Mean Years of Education	5.26	31	52.85	54.92
Tourism	Cultural & Natu-ral Beauty[1]	4.63	5	7.26	4.70

1. Amount: Refers to score on a scale for Tourism Sector
2. Relative Rank: Strength of asset compared to other countries
3. Sector Share: Share of value added of total GDP that was added by sector

Table 18
Country: Latvia
Growth in GDP Per Capita in the period 1995 – 2007:
164.77%

Sector	Asset	Amount	Rela-tive Rank[2]	Sec-tor Share 95[3]	Sector Share 07

Agricul-ture	KM2 arable land PC	0.004	10	8.90	3.74
Forestry	KM2 forest land PC	0.013	8	2.44	0.96
Industry	% of Population Unschooled	0.4	38	30.26	24.53
Services	Mean Years of Education	8.99	9	60.84	71.73
Tourism	Cultural & Natu-ral Beauty[1]	2.55	31	0.61	2.79

1. Amount: Refers to score on a scale for Tourism Sector
2. Relative Rank: Strength of asset compared to other countries
3. Sector Share: Share of value added of total GDP that was added by sector

Table 19
Country: Lithuania
Growth in GDP Per Capita in the period 1995 – 2007:
142.90%

Sector	Asset	Amount	Rela-tive Rank[2]	Sector Share 95[3]	Sector Share 07
Agricul-ture	KM2 arable land PC	0.008	1	11.05	3.87
Forestry	KM2 forest land PC	0.005	17	1.35	0.37
Industry	% of Population Unschooled	5.7	25	31.52	32.95
Services	Mean Years of Education	9.17	7	57.43	63.18
Tourism	Cultural & Natural Beauty[1]	2.44	32	1.19	2.90

1. Amount: Refers to score on a scale for Tourism Sector
2. Relative Rank: Strength of asset compared to other countries
3. Sector Share: Share of value added of total GDP that was added by sector

Table 20
Country: Malaysia
Growth in GDP Per Capita in the period 1995 – 2007: 42.69%

Sector	Asset	Amount	Rela-tive Rank[2]	Sector Share 95[3]	Sector Share 07
Agricul-ture	KM2 arable land PC	0.000	38	12.95	9.99
Forestry	KM2 forest land PC	0.011	10	9.33	4.51
Industry	% of Population Unschooled	13.4	16	41.40	42.22
Services	Mean Years of Education	8.39	14	45.65	47.80
Tourism	Cultural & Natural Beauty[1]	4.09	12	5.69	9.27

1. Amount: Refers to score on a scale for Tourism Sector
2. Relative Rank: Strength of asset compared to other countries
3. Sector Share: Share of value added of total GDP that was added by sector

Table 21
Country: Mauritius
Growth in GDP Per Capita in the period 1995 – 2007: 59.93%

Sector	Asset	Amount	Relative Rank[2]	Sector Share 95[3]	Sector Share 07
Agriculture	KM2 arable land PC	0.001	33	10.38	4.93
Forestry	KM2 forest land PC	0.000	36	0.01	0.01
Industry	% of Population Unschooled	10.4	20	32.03	25.38
Services	Mean Years of Education	6.83	24	57.59	69.69
Tourism	Cultural & Natural Beauty[1]	2.03	37	15.38	20.91

1. Amount: Refers to score on a scale for Tourism Sector
2. Relative Rank: Strength of asset compared to other countries
3. Sector Share: Share of value added of total GDP that was added by sector

Table 22
Country: Mexico
Growth in GDP Per Capita in the period 1995 – 2007: 25.68%

Sector	Asset	Amount	Relative Rank[2]	Sector Share 95[3]	Sector Share 07
Agriculture	KM2 arable land PC	0.002	23	4.37	3.32
Forestry	KM2 forest land PC	0.007	14	0.19	0.07

Industry	% of Population Unschooled	12.9	17	32.47	36.10
Services	Mean Years of Education	7.20	23	63.16	60.58
Tourism	Cultural & Natural Beauty[1]	5.18	2	2.73	1.35

1. Amount: Refers to score on a scale for Tourism Sector
2. Relative Rank: Strength of asset compared to other countries
3. Sector Share: Share of value added of total GDP that was added by sector

Table 23
Country: Moldova
Growth in GDP Per Capita in the period 1995 – 2007: 37.74%

Sector	Asset	Amount	Relative Rank[2]	Sector Share 95[3]	Sector Share 07
Agriculture	KM2 arable land PC	0.005	5	33.02	12.01
Forestry	KM2 forest land PC	0.001	33	0.28	0.15
Industry	% of Population Unschooled	7.4	22	32.15	17.15
Services	Mean Years of Education	8.89	10	34.83	70.84
Tourism	Cultural & Natural Beauty[1]	1.75	38	3.97	6.23

1. Amount: Refers to score on a scale for Tourism Sector
2. Relative Rank: Strength of asset compared to other countries
3. Sector Share: Share of value added of total GDP that was added by sector

Table 24
Country: Morocco
Growth in GDP Per Capita in the period 1995 – 2007: 50.46%

Sector	Asset	Amount	Rela-tive Rank[2]	Sector Share 95[3]	Sector Share 07
Agriculture	KM2 arable land PC	0.003	17	15.36	12.20
Forestry	KM2 forest land PC	0.002	26	0.28	0.13
Industry	% of Population Unschooled	59.4	2	29.98	27.70
Services	Mean Years of Education	3.82	36	54.66	60.10
Tourism	Cultural & Natural Beauty[1]	3.11	22	4.40	11.99

1. Amount: Refers to score on a scale for Tourism Sector
2. Relative Rank: Strength of asset compared to other countries
3. Sector Share: Share of value added of total GDP that was added by sector

Table 25
Country: Namibia
Growth in GDP Per Capita in the period 1995 – 2007: 37.05%

Sector	Asset	Amount	Rela-tive Rank[2]	Sector Share 95[3]	Sector Share 07
Agriculture	KM2 arable land PC	0.005	4	10.61	9.22
Forestry	KM2 forest land PC	0.051	3	0.51	0.55

Industry	% of Population Unschooled	22.5	11	24.44	34.77
Services	Mean Years of Education	6.05	27	64.94	56.01
Tourism	Cultural & Natural Beauty[1]	3.94	14	7.23	7.77

1. Amount: Refers to score on a scale for Tourism Sector
2. Relative Rank: Strength of asset compared to other countries
3. Sector Share: Share of value added of total GDP that was added by sector

Table 26
Country: Nicaragua
Growth in GDP Per Capita in the period 1995 – 2007: 36.68%

Sector	Asset	Amount	Rela-tive Rank[2]	Sector Share 95[3]	Sector Share 07
Agricul-ture	KM2 arable land PC	0.004	12	22.59	17.97
Forestry	KM2 forest land PC	0.009	13	1.99	1.23
Industry	% of Population Unschooled	32.1	7	22.60	22.90
Services	Mean Years of Education	5.02	33	54.81	58.79
Tourism	Cultural & Natural Beauty[1]	3.21	20	1.34	3.06

1. Amount: Refers to score on a scale for Tourism Sector
2. Relative Rank: Strength of asset compared to other countries
3. Sector Share: Share of value added of total GDP that was added by sector

Table 27
Country: Panama
Growth in GDP Per Capita in the period 1995 – 2007: 51.90%

Sector	Asset	Amount	Rela-tive Rank[2]	Sector Share 95[3]	Sector Share 07
Agricul-ture	KM2 arable land PC	0.002	26	6.76	5.34
Forestry	KM2 forest land PC	0.018	6	0.24	0.12
Industry	% of Population Unschooled	8.2	21	23.56	19.22
Services	Mean Years of Education	8.43	13	70.27	75.44
Tourism	Cultural & Natural Beauty[1]	4.34	10	3.27	8.52

1. Amount: Refers to score on a scale for Tourism Sector
2. Relative Rank: Strength of asset compared to other countries
3. Sector Share: Share of value added of total GDP that was added by sector

Table 28
Country: Peru
Growth in GDP Per Capita in the period 1995 – 2007: 38.91%

Sector	Asset	Amount	Rela-tive Rank[2]	Sector Share 95[3]	Sector Share 07
Agricul-ture	KM2 arable land PC	0.002	28	8.93	7.31
Forestry	KM2 forest land PC	0.032	5	0.28	0.20

Industry	% of Population Unschooled	12.6	18	32.31	41.11
Services	Mean Years of Education	7.88	17	58.76	51.58
Tourism	Cultural & Natural Beauty[1]	4.61	6	1.04	2.05

1. Amount: Refers to score on a scale for Tourism Sector
2. Relative Rank: Strength of asset compared to other countries
3. Sector Share: Share of value added of total GDP that was added by sector

Table 29
Country: Philippines
Growth in GDP Per Capita in the period 1995 – 2007: 31.33%

Sector	Asset	Amount	Relative Rank[2]	Sector Share 95[3]	Sector Share 07
Agriculture	KM2 arable land PC	0.001	34	21.63	12.50
Forestry	KM2 forest land PC	0.001	32	0.60	0.34
Industry	% of Population Unschooled	5.3	26	32.06	33.05
Services	Mean Years of Education	7.56	21	46.31	54.45
Tourism	Cultural & Natural Beauty[1]	3.39	18	1.55	5.16

1. Amount: Refers to score on a scale for Tourism Sector
2. Relative Rank: Strength of asset compared to other countries
3. Sector Share: Share of value added of total GDP that was added by sector

Table 30
Country: Poland
Growth in GDP Per Capita in the period 1995 – 2007: 73.12%

Sector	Asset	Amount	Rela-tive Rank[2]	Sector Share 95[3]	Sector Share 07
Agricul-ture	KM2 arable land PC	0.004	11	5.47	3.44
Forestry	KM2 forest land PC	0.002	25	0.27	0.19
Industry	% of Population Unschooled	2.2	33	36.40	33.19
Services	Mean Years of Education	9.86	5	58.13	63.36
Tourism	Cultural & Natural Beauty[1]	3.14	21	4.45	2.71

1. Amount: Refers to score on a scale for Tourism Sector
2. Relative Rank: Strength of asset compared to other countries
3. Sector Share: Share of value added of total GDP that was added by sector

Table 31
Country: Romania
Growth in GDP Per Capita in the period 1995 – 2007: 63.83%

Sector	Asset	Amount	Rela-tive Rank[2]	Sector Share 95[3]	Sector Share 07
Agricul-ture	KM2 arable land PC	0.004	8	19.15	5.47
Forestry	KM2 forest land PC	0.003	21	0.66	0.22

Industry	% of Population Unschooled	3.8	32	38.37	36.67
Services	Mean Years of Education	9.70	6	42.48	57.86
Tourism	Cultural & Natural Beauty[1]	2.7	27	1.87	1.40

1. Amount: Refers to score on a scale for Tourism Sector
2. Relative Rank: Strength of asset compared to other countries
3. Sector Share: Share of value added of total GDP that was added by sector

Table 32
Country: Senegal
Growth in GDP Per Capita in the period 1995 – 2007: 20.87%

Sector	Asset	Amount	Relative Rank[2]	Sector Share 95[3]	Sector Share 07
Agriculture	KM2 arable land PC	0.004	14	21.01	13.77
Forestry	KM2 forest land PC	0.010	11	4.11	2.66
Industry	% of Population Unschooled	60.5	1	23.78	24.12
Services	Mean Years of Education	2.20	38	55.21	62.11
Tourism	Cultural & Natural Beauty[1]	3.04	23	3.45	5.51

1. Amount: Refers to score on a scale for Tourism Sector
2. Relative Rank: Strength of asset compared to other countries
3. Sector Share: Share of value added of total GDP that was added by sector

Table 33
Country: Slovak Republic
Growth in GDP Per Capita in the period 1995 – 2007: 82.42%

Sector	Asset	Amount	Rela-tive Rank[2]	Sector Share 95[3]	Sector Share 07
Agricul-ture	KM2 arable land PC	0.003	20	5.63	4.00
Forestry	KM2 forest land PC	0.004	19	0.42	0.23
Industry	% of Population Unschooled	1.8	34	36.82	37.87
Services	Mean Years of Education	11.24	2	57.54	58.13
Tourism	Cultural & Natural Beauty[1]	3.31	19	3.26	2.72

1. Amount: Refers to score on a scale for Tourism Sector
2. Relative Rank: Strength of asset compared to other countries
3. Sector Share: Share of value added of total GDP that was added by sector

Table 34
Country: South Africa
Growth in GDP Per Capita in the period 1995 – 2007: 30.56%

Sector	Asset	Amount	Rela-tive Rank[2]	Sector Share 95[3]	Sector Share 07
Agricul-ture	KM2 arable land PC	0.003	15	3.86	2.96
Forestry	KM2 forest land PC	0.002	24	1.00	0.64

Industry	% of Population Unschooled	5.2	27	34.87	29.69
Services	Mean Years of Education	8.29	15	61.27	67.35
Tourism	Cultural & Natural Beauty[1]	4.28	11	1.71	3.41

1. Amount: Refers to score on a scale for Tourism Sector
2. Relative Rank: Strength of asset compared to other countries
3. Sector Share: Share of value added of total GDP that was added by sector

Table 35
Country: Thailand
Growth in GDP Per Capita in the period 1995 – 2007: 33.56%

Sector	Asset	Amount	Relative Rank[2]	Sector Share 95[3]	Sector Share 07
Agriculture	KM2 arable land PC	0.003	21	9.08	9.35
Forestry	KM2 forest land PC	0.003	22	0.34	0.58
Industry	% of Population Unschooled	11.8	19	37.53	39.55
Services	Mean Years of Education	5.50	29	53.39	51.10
Tourism	Cultural & Natural Beauty[1]	4.47	7	5.47	7.83

1. Amount: Refers to score on a scale for Tourism Sector
2. Relative Rank: Strength of asset compared to other countries
3. Sector Share: Share of value added of total GDP that was added by sector

Table 36
Country: Tunisia
Growth in GDP Per Capita in the period 1995 – 2007: 58.17%

Sector	Asset	Amount	Rela-tive Rank[2]	Sector Share 95[3]	Sector Share 07
Agricul-ture	KM2 arable land PC	0.003	19	13.04	9.40
Forestry	KM2 forest land PC	0.001	34	0.17	0.09
Industry	% of Population Unschooled	37.8	5	33.72	31.18
Services	Mean Years of Education	5.07	32	53.24	59.42
Tourism	Cultural & Natural Beauty[1]	2.36	34	10.34	8.63

1. Amount: Refers to score on a scale for Tourism Sector
2. Relative Rank: Strength of asset compared to other countries
3. Sector Share: Share of value added of total GDP that was added by sector

Table 37
Country: Turkey
Growth in GDP Per Capita in the period 1995 – 2007: 43.50%

Sector	Asset	Amount	Rela-tive Rank[2]	Sector Share 95[3]	Sector Share 07
Agricul-ture	KM2 arable land PC	0.004	7	16.29	8.53
Forestry	KM2 forest land PC	0.002	28	0.18	0.07

Industry	% of Population Unschooled	23.8	10	33.24	29.85
Services	Mean Years of Education	5.44	30	50.47	63.73
Tourism	Cultural & Natural Beauty[1]	2.78	25	2.70	3.33

1. Amount: Refers to score on a scale for Tourism Sector
2. Relative Rank: Strength of asset compared to other countries
3. Sector Share: Share of value added of total GDP that was added by sector

Table 38
Country: Uruguay
Growth in GDP Per Capita in the period 1995 – 2007: 24.49%

Sector	Asset	Amount	Relative Rank[2]	Sector Share 95[3]	Sector Share 07
Agriculture	KM2 arable land PC	0.004	9	8.62	9.88
Forestry	KM2 forest land PC	0.003	20	0.45	1.15
Industry	% of Population Unschooled	4.2	30	28.92	27.49
Services	Mean Years of Education	7.57	20	62.46	62.63
Tourism	Cultural & Natural Beauty[1]	2.4	33	3.93	3.89

1. Amount: Refers to score on a scale for Tourism Sector
2. Relative Rank: Strength of asset compared to other countries
3. Sector Share: Share of value added of total GDP that was added by sector